ANDREWS

NOTES

including
- *Life of the Author*
- *Introduction*
- *List of Characters*
- *Summaries and Commentaries*
- *Character Analyses*
- *Review Questions*
- *Selected Bibliography*

by
Michael B. Mavor

INCORPORATED

LINCOLN, NEBRASKA 68501

Editor

Gary Carey, M.A.
University of Colorado

Consulting Editor

James L. Roberts, Ph.D.
Department of English
University of Nebraska

ISBN 0-8220-0682-0
© Copyright 1971
by
Cliffs Notes, Inc.
All Rights Reserved
Printed in U.S.A.

1997 Printing

The Cliffs Notes logo, the names "Cliffs" and "Cliffs Notes," and the black and yellow diagonal-stripe cover design are all registered trademarks belonging to Cliffs Notes, Inc., and may not be used in whole or in part without written permission.

Cliffs Notes, Inc.   Lincoln, Nebraska

CONTENTS

Life of the Author 5

Introduction to *Joseph Andrews* 8
    Form 9
    Characterization 10
    Style 11
    Moral Tone 12

List of Characters 13

Summaries and Commentaries
    Author's Preface 15
    Book I 17
    Book II 33
    Book III 50
    Book IV 59

Character Analyses
    Joseph Andrews 68
    Fanny 69
    Lady Booby 69
    Mrs. Slipslop 70
    Parson Adams 70

Review Questions 71

Selected Bibliography 72

Joseph Andrews Notes

LIFE OF THE AUTHOR

Henry Fielding was born in 1707 into a family that was essentially aristocratic. His mother's father was a justice of the Queen's Bench, while his paternal grandfather was an archdeacon of Salisbury; in these two men there may have been something of the genesis of Fielding's bent toward the law, his great love of learning, and his firm sense of Christian morality. Fielding's father, Sir Edmund Fielding, a colonel of aristocratic descent, married Sarah Gould in 1706; it was a "runaway" marriage, and the sober Henry Gould excluded Sir Edmund from the estate which he left his daughter. When Sarah died in 1718, Fielding's father entered into a long battle with the maternal side of the family over the estate. What there was of the rake in his father was inherited by Fielding; their spirit is that of Tom Jones, whose isolation when young also reflects the early death of Fielding's mother and the ensuing divisions in the family. Both *Joseph Andrews* and *Tom Jones* portray a young man on the move until he is brought to a secure standstill by the revelation of his true identity.

After attending Eton College, where he was exposed to the classical authors he came to love so much, Fielding joined his father in London and, in 1728, wrote his first play; nearly thirty more were to come from his pen in the next nine years. This was the period when the rake was to the fore in his character; the dismal account of Mr. Wilson's dissipations in London (*Joseph Andrews*, Book III, Chapter 3) represents a stern warning from an experienced Fielding about the dangers of city life. Before the city completely enveloped him, however, Fielding spent a short spell abroad at the University of Leiden in Holland. He returned to London in the fall of 1729. It was not a time of great theater, but there was much material for parody and satire, and Fielding exercised his talents with such verve, particularly in the political field, that in 1737 the harassed Prime Minister, Sir Robert Walpole, introduced a Theatrical Licensing Act. Fielding wrote no more for the stage, but his novels are richer because of his experience as a playwright. The incidents of burlesque humor in *Joseph Andrews*, the concealment scenes in *Tom Jones*, and the authentic patterns and rhythms of dialogue attest to Fielding's theatrical background.

At a loss for a job, Fielding took up the study of law at the Middle Temple five months after the passage of Walpole's Licensing Act. With his outlet for playwriting quelled, Fielding had to support himself somehow, for he had married Charlotte Craddock in 1734, and they were always short of money. (Charlotte, critics believe, was almost certainly the model for Fielding's portraits of the ideal woman: Amelia, Sophia, and, from *Joseph Andrews*, possibly Fanny Goodwill and Mrs. Wilson.) From playwriting Fielding turned to journalism. From 1739 to 1741 he edited a satirically political newspaper, *The Champion;* the writing is quite admirable, and we can see a more serious Fielding emerging as the issues of the day come under his scrutiny.

In 1740, Fielding was called to the Bar, but success as a magistrate lay far in the future; at this time, chance joined hands with Fielding's rich experience as a dramatist and a journalist to change the course both of his own life and that of the novel; in 1740, Samuel Richardson published *Pamela, or Virtue Rewarded*. The novel was an immediate success—with almost everyone but Fielding. Fielding objected to the discrepancy between the expressed morality of "virtue rewarded" and the sexual content in the novel. Perhaps because he was poor and had two young children to provide for, he decided to try and make some money with a parody of *Pamela*. Whatever the reason, in 1741, he published his riotous and bawdy *An Apology for the Life of Mrs. Shamela Andrews*. In it, Shamela is a fortune-hunter who uses her "virtue" in a thoroughly lecherous and mercenary way. The theme is one of disguise and pretense, and it is just this theme which is continued in *Joseph Andrews*, published in 1742.

The years surrounding the publication of *Joseph Andrews* were hard ones for Fielding. The death of his father in June, 1741, left him sorrowful, and none the richer, and in March of 1742 his favorite daughter died. In June, 1741, Fielding also severed his connection with *The Champion;* his disaffection with the Patriots, as they were called, is perhaps reflected in his comments on "patriotism" in *Joseph Andrews* (Book II, Chapter 9). As a result of his literary and political notoriety, it was difficult for Fielding to get ahead in the legal profession, and his last two novels, *Tom Jones* and *Amelia*, occasionally reflect the anguish of a man who knows that he has brought wretchedness and poverty to the woman he loves. Yet if Fielding could not get money by practicing law, he did use the subject of law in his writing; *Jonathan Wild*, which was published in 1743, is filled with biting accounts of the grotesque malpractices in the system of criminal law. In 1744, Fielding's wife died and, for a time, Fielding's friends thought that he would lose his mind. But he took up his political pen again and wrote for the anti-Jacobite journal, *The True Patriot*. In 1747, he married Mary Daniel, who had been a maid to his wife and had shared his grief when Charlotte died. From this time, his fortunes began to brighten. In 1748, he was appointed Justice of the Peace for Westminster and, subsequently, he was made magistrate of all Middlesex, and in 1749 *Tom Jones* appeared. The concept of good nature which played such an important part in *Joseph Andrews* is also central to this novel. At one point, Squire Allworthy comments that Tom, despite his many misdemeanors, has a heart of gold: "I am convinced, my child, that you have much goodness, generosity, and honor, in your temper: if you will add prudence and religion to these, you must be happy." One is never quite convinced that Tom becomes either prudent or religious, but the happy ending illustrated that Fielding the artist is again practicing the positive outlook he advocates. Tom and Sophia are optimistically left to "preserve the purest and tenderest affection for each other, an affection daily increased and confirmed by mutual endearments, and mutual esteem."

This optimism is hardly the case with Captain and Mrs. Booth in *Amelia* (1751). Captain Booth's weaknesses are an echo of Fielding's own, while Amelia, with her tolerance, patience, and love, is probably another portrait of Fielding's first wife, Charlotte. At one point, Amelia, having made her husband a dish of hashed mutton for his supper, feels thirsty, but denies herself half a pint of wine to save sixpence, "while her husband was paying a debt of several guineas, incurred by the ace of trumps being in the hands of his adversary." Amelia is clearly a nearly perfect heroine and glows with a tender warmth against the grim descriptions of life in Newgate prison, where Captain Booth is committed at the beginning of the book. His rescue by Miss Matthews, an elegant courtesan, is a continual irritant, but Fielding eventually rescues the Booths from their domestic difficulties with the discovery that Amelia is an heiress. This turn of events, however, does not obliterate the harsh details of Newgate and London society which permeate the rest of the book. Henry Fielding's three best novels, it has been said, are all composed of a certain "fluctuation from assent to refusal."

Fielding's health was not good; he was terribly overworked and, in the summer of 1754, he went by sea to Lisbon with his wife and daughter. Though the voyage resulted in a diary published posthumously as *A Journal of a Voyage to Lisbon*, the quest for good health was in vain; he died on October 8, 1754, at the age of forty-seven.

INTRODUCTION TO *JOSEPH ANDREWS*

In *Joseph Andrews*, Fielding the author, magistrate, and moralist refuses to accept much of what he sees around him; in Book III, he states that his purpose is "to hold the glass to thousands in their closets, that they may contemplate their deformity, and endeavour to reduce it." But just as Fielding excludes the burlesque, which makes up the entirety of *Shamela*, from his "sentiments and characters" in *Joseph Andrews*, so too does he progress beyond a mere criticism of the "ridiculous" to a positive statement and portrayal of the values in which he believed. We find that we are no longer merely laughing *at* people and situations, but also laughing *with* them; we are taking delight, rather than laughing in scorn. Our sense of delight at the close of *Joseph Andrews* is in no sense destructive, but represents one of the many aspects of this book which can be considered under such headings as form, characterization, style, and moral tone.

FORM

Joseph Andrews is a picaresque novel of the road; the title page tells us that it was "Written in Imitation of the Manner of CERVANTES, Author of *Don Quixote*." Despite its looseness of construction, however, *Joseph Andrews* does make a deliberate move from the confusion and hypocrisy of London to the open sincerity of the country; one might perhaps apply Fielding's own words in a review he wrote of Charlotte Lennox's *The Female Quixote:* "...here is a regular story, which, though possibly it is not pursued with that epic regularity which would give it the name of an action, comes nearer to that perfection than the loose unconnected adventures in *Don Quixote;* of which you may transverse the order as you please, without an injury to the whole."

This journey is undertaken in more than a simply geographical sense. Fielding takes his characters through a series of confusing episodes, finally aligning them with their correct partners in an improved social setting, from which the most recalcitrant characters are excluded; the characters, for the most part, have all measured and achieved a greater degree of self-knowledge. Thus the marriage of Fanny to a more experienced Joseph takes place in an ideal setting—the country—and is facilitated by the generosity of an enlightened Mr. Booby. Lady Booby, unchanged and unreformed, returns to London, excluding herself from the society which Fielding has reshaped.

It is often the business of comedy to correct excess, and Fielding has not spared the devious practices of a lawyer Scout, or the boorish greed of a Parson Trulliber. But his comedy includes a sense of delight, and the order into which he molds

Joseph Andrews is a positive affirmation of the qualities of love, charity, and sincerity, expressed by Adams, Joseph, and Fanny.

CHARACTERIZATION

It is the *active* virtue (in Adams' case, it is flawed by just the right amount of vanity and inconsistency) of Adams, Joseph, and Fanny that redeems this book from the flock of hypocrites that peoples its pages. Indeed, Fielding explains in his preface that he has made Adams a clergyman "since no other office could have given him so many opportunities of displaying his worthy inclinations." It is important we realize that despite Joseph and Fanny remaining *types*, as do all the other characters, Adams emerges as an *individual*. He is a positive force not only as a clergyman who puts his principles of charity into practice, but as a man who applies himself to Aeschylus for comfort, as well as to his pipe and ale, manages to confront the physical obstacles of the world in the most awkward ways, prides himself rather too much as a teacher of Latin and as a writer of sermons, and takes people absolutely at face value. He not only fits into the positive side of Fielding's comic pattern, but emerges as a "round" and fully developed character who reinforces his goodness by his humanity.

The other characters are "flat"; they are types, rather than individuals, and are depicted by an emphasis on a single characteristic; greediness sums up Mrs. Tow-wouse, while Mrs. Slipslop comes to life through her malapropisms. "I describe not men, but manners; not an individual, but a species," Fielding states in Book III, Chapter 1; portraying people as types enables him to include them more easily in his comic visions; we can more easily survey the eccentricities of the rest of the species, using our detachment (Adams' detachment) to place and criticize them.

There are two important points to be made about Fielding's method of characterization. First, when asked about the province of the novel as a genre, most people would probably reply in terms of "the real, the actual, and the everyday." Consider what Fielding does. All of the characters in *Joseph Andrews*, with one exception, reveal themselves in a realistic and vividly portrayed setting. The exception, of course, is Parson Adams, who exists in the same world, but does not relate to it and, in this way, he becomes a positive force. It is the task of the novelist to convey the actual flavor of life, but there is a place for idealism as well as realism. Just as Fielding's control gives an order to the fragments of real life, so Adams' naivete and innocence add an extra dimension to the strong sense of actuality conveyed in *Joseph Andrews*.

The second point concerns the idea of appearance. In real life we must always judge people by externals; the novel, however, offers an extra dimension. In the novel, we can penetrate the facades and see what people are really thinking, whereas in real life we have only the evidence of their words and actions. This is not a process in which Fielding indulges himself, however; his dramatic instinct often has his characters confront each other in much the same way that they might in real life. The characters may be deceived by or mistaken about each other, but the theme of appearance versus reality is communicated to the reader. Fielding clearly shows us how difficult it is to penetrate through the trappings to the heart of man.

STYLE

Although Fielding's description of his work as a "comic romance" or "comic epic-poem in prose" introduces the elements of parody and burlesque, certain qualities of the epic itself, and romance, do inject themselves into *Joseph Andrews*. These are the qualities of imagination, idealism, and a happy conclusion, all of which serve to underscore Fielding's purpose in writing this book. In his preface, Fielding is careful to disassociate himself from the "productions of romance writers," yet it must be admitted that the end of *Joseph Andrews*, with its accounts of gypsies and changeling babies, has certain elements of the fairy tale come true. In fact, Fielding's achievement is to superimpose this positive act of imagination on the raw material of the very real world. His achievement, in Samuel Johnson's words, "may be termed, not improperly, the comedy of romance, and is to be conducted nearly by the rules of comic poetry," terms remarkably similar to Fielding's own. This "comedy of romance" requires, Johnson claims, "together with that learning which is to be gained from books, that experience which can never be attained by solitary diligence, but must arise from general converse and accurate observation of the living world." It is this combination of the raw and the refined, of the real and the ideal, that Fielding has created in his "comic epic-poem in prose."

MORAL TONE

Fielding maintains a positive outlook in the book, emphasizing charitable and virtuous *action*. Adams is a pugilistic parson, and both he and Joseph always act on their beliefs, defending them by force if necessary. Adams is offended by the insipid Methodist doctrine of faith against good works; to him, human beings distinguish themselves by what they do: "a virtuous and good Turk, or heathen, are more acceptable in the sight of their Creator than a vicious and wicked Christian, though his faith was as perfectly orthodox as St. Paul's himself." In a similar vein, Fielding advocates through Joseph a degree of control. Joseph's self-restraint contrasts with Lady Booby's turbulent passion, on which her reason has little effect. But Fielding's treatment is always warm; Lady Booby, for example, is not savagely condemned; Fielding's reason is not Swift's. In *Joseph Andrews*, Fielding has written with both his head *and* his heart; he has refused some things and assented warmly to others so that the positive delight which we take in a book that admittedly has echoes of Shamela shows how far he has travelled in his literary craft.

LIST OF CHARACTERS

Joseph Andrews

A handsome young fellow who battles for his virginity throughout the novel.

Gaffar and Gammar Andrews

Parents of Pamela and, it is believed, of Joseph.

Mr. Booby

The nephew of Sir Thomas Booby.

Sir Thomas Booby

The deceased husband of Lady Booby.

Lady Booby

A hot-blooded young widow who tries every way possible to seduce Joseph.

Mrs. Slipslop

A repulsive servant woman who also pursues Joseph.

Peter Pounce

The steward to Lady Booby.

Mr. Abraham Adams

A charitable curate.

Frances (Fanny) Goodwill

A beautiful young country girl; Joseph's beloved.

The Wilsons

The real parents of Joseph Andrews.

Lady Tittle ⎫
Lady Tattle ⎭ two gossips.

Plain Tim

A good-hearted host.

Postillion

A generous fellow who offers Joseph an overcoat to cover his nakedness.

Mr. Tow-wouse

A bumbling, good-natured innkeeper.

Mrs. Tow-wouse

The greedy wife of the innkeeper.

Betty

A warm-hearted chambermaid.

Barnabas

A punch-drinking clergyman.

Tom Suckbribe

The constable.

Leonora

A silly young girl who loses two lovers because of her vacillations.

Horatio

A suitor who has no money but much love for Leonora.

Bellarmine

A suitor who has little love for Leonora but who hopes to inherit her father's fortune.

Lindamira

A gossip.

Mrs. Grave-airs

A prude.

Parson Trulliber

A hypocritical country parson.

The Pedlar (peddler)

The man who reveals the secret of Joseph's parentage.

Lawyer Scout

An unscrupulous lawyer.

Mrs. Adams

Parson Adams' disagreeable wife.

SUMMARIES AND COMMENTARIES

AUTHOR'S PREFACE

Summary

Fielding sets out to define his terms and to differentiate *Joseph Andrews* from the "productions of romance writers on the one hand, and burlesque writers on the other." He admits that he has included some elements of burlesque in his "comic epic-poem in prose," but excludes them from the sentiments and the characters because burlesque in writing, like "Caricatura" in painting, exhibits "monsters, not men." True comedy, however, finds its source in nature: "life everywhere furnishes an accurate observer with the ridiculous." The source of the true ridiculous is affectation, which can usually be traced to either vanity or hypocrisy. The latter, he points out, is the more striking as it involves a measure of deceit over and above the mere ostentation of vanity. Fielding defends the various vices inserted in his novel because "they are never the principal figure." He closes by emphasizing the character of Parson Adams, "whose goodness of heart stems from his "perfect simplicity."

Commentary

As in his later novel, *Tom Jones*, Fielding provides the reader with a critical framework and a kind of "Bill of Fare to the Feast." The classics are as important to Fielding as they are to Parson Adams, and in constructing the definition of *Joseph Andrews* as a "comic epic poem in prose," Fielding refers to two works which help explain his own. The reference to the *Odyssey* prepares the reader for the themes of wandering and faithfulness, but whereas in the *Odyssey* the much-tried hero is pursued on his homeward travels by Poseidon's wrath, in Fénelon's version in *Télémaque* (also referred to in the preface), it is Venus who is the vengeful deity. Thus, one is prepared for the pursuit of Joseph by Lady Booby and—in the intervals—by Mrs. Slipslop.

It is vital to appreciate the limited role that Fielding gives to burlesque; he is attempting to describe the real nature of comedy, just as Joseph Andrews will attempt to discover the real nature of everyone and everything. In linking himself with Hogarth, the "comic history" painter whose works are in the "exactest copying of nature," Fielding presents an argument later echoed by Henry James: "The only reason for the existence of a novel is that it does attempt to represent life. When it relinquishes this attempt, the same attempt that we see on the canvas of the painter, it will have arrived at a very strange pass" ("The

Art of Fiction," 1884). Fielding also associates himself with Ben Jonson, "who of all men understood the Ridiculous the best," yet, it would be a mistake to view *Joseph Andrews* as merely a bitter, corrective piece of satire. The final reference to Parson Adams, for example, establishes the sort of unadorned criterion of simplicity against which the vanity and the hypocrisy of most of the other characters will be measured. In addition, Adams' character as a *clergyman* is important; throughout the novel, Fielding will be leading his readers beyond "vulgar opinion," which establishes the characters of men according to their dress rather than their greater excellencies, to a recognition of the "unaccommodated man" *(King Lear)* whom Lear described as "the thing itself."

The existence of the preface, the careful definition of terms, the reference to painting and to the "circle of incidents," and the promise of a happy outcome all indicate the extent to which Fielding is in control of his novel. The characters may, like Adams, have a life of their own, but it is the essence of humanity, distilled through Fielding's own vision, which is presented to us: "I describe not men, but manners; not an individual, but a species" (Book III, Chapter 1). Already we are aware of his acute discernments, his breadth of vision, his firm sense of organization, and his belief in the essential goodness of human nature. The vices for which he apologizes in the preface are more than balanced by the character of Adams and by the fact that they are "accidental consequences of some human frailty or foible."

BOOK I

Chapter 1

Summary

Fielding tells us that examples are often better teachers than precepts and thus he defends the practice of biography, claiming that such books communicate valuable patterns of virtue to a wide public. He lists several biographies, including those of Colley Cibber and Pamela Andrews, as examples of male virtue and female chastity. Fielding reinforces his opening argument and introduces his own work by remarking that it was by keeping his sister's excellent example of virtue before him that Joseph Andrews was able to preserve his own purity.

Commentary

Whatever the conduct of Joseph Andrews may prove to be, the virtue of chastity did *not* belong to Colley Cibber. This is made clear by the cutting remark that concludes the opening chapter. In this way, Fielding launches immediately on his main theme—that is, the discrepancy between appearance and reality—by mocking Colley Cibber, who in his autobiography called Fielding "a broken wit." In this way, Fielding throws a shadow on Pamela's chastity also, and we see that the genesis of *Joseph Andrews* is due to Fielding's hatred of hypocrisy.

Chapters 2-3

Summary

When he was ten years old, young Joey Andrews served as bird-keeper and "whipper-in" of the pack of hounds of Sir Thomas Booby. Unfortunately, however, he was soon removed to the stables because the "sweetness" of his voice, instead of scaring the birds and controlling the dogs, attracted them both. His success and honesty in racing Sir Thomas' horses brought Joey to the notice of Lady Booby, whose attendant he became at the age of seventeen. One of his duties was to bear the lady's prayer book to church, and there his fine singing drew the attention of the curate, Mr. Abraham Adams.

Adams is not only an excellent scholar, but "a man of good sense, good parts, and good nature." However, at the same time, he is naive, and his economic position is encumbered by a wife and six children. Adams questions Joey and is so impressed by his wide reading, his diligence and candor that he decides to approach Lady Booby about teaching the boy Latin. As Lady Booby looks on Adams as a kind of domestic, his only means of access to her is through her waiting-gentlewoman, Mrs. Slipslop. There he learns that Joey will soon be taken to London by Lady Booby.

Commentary

The mocking way in which Fielding treats the "sacred" data of biography shows that he wants to move straight to the heart of the matter; Joey's virtues are more important than his ancestors. He is described as being attractive, able, and honest; the fearlessness with which he manages the most spirited horses is an indication of his control and self-discipline.

Adams is impressed by Joey's innocence and industry. These qualities, along with the childlike simplicity of the parson, contrast with the way Sir Thomas judges men by "their dress or fortune," and with the vanity of Mrs. Slipslop in her tortuous speech, which leaves the straightforward Adams completely befuddled. As for Lady Booby, she is vain enough to speak of Adams as a "kind of domestic only" and her country neighbors as "the brutes."

Chapter 4

Summary

Now in London with Lady Booby, Joey is influenced, at least outwardly, by the fashions of the city, and Lady Booby begins to find him more attractive than ever. Her familiarities with Joey become the subject of drawing room gossip, thanks to Lady Tittle and Lady Tattle, but Joey remains essentially unaffected: "if he was outwardly a pretty fellow, his morals remained entirely uncorrupted.

Commentary

The hints given about town life in Chapter 3 are now expanded; London becomes the center of intrigue and affectation. In the same way that the trials and tribulations of this world affect Parson Adams only temporarily and in terms of appearance, so Joey's decadence is only superficial. The roots of Lady Booby's burgeoning affections run deeper.

Chapters 5-10

Summary

The death of Sir Thomas Booby confines Lady Booby to her house for a period of mourning, but she soon begins to pursue Joseph. Calling him to her bedside, she cunningly tries to arouse his passions, but fails. She cannot understand Joseph's innocence and his failure to understand her. Joseph, somewhat perturbed, writes a letter to his sister, Pamela. He thinks that Lady Booby is *perhaps* pursuing him, but charitably ascribes this to distraction over the death of Sir Thomas. In any case, he anticipates his dismissal and advises Pamela of his return to the Booby country-seat. After sealing the letter, he runs into Mrs. Slipslop who has long nursed a secret passion for Joseph. Provoked by Joseph's inability to understand her advances, she is about to seize her prey when her mistress's bell rings. Joseph is temporarily saved.

Fielding, drawing the reader's attention to the different manifestations of love in Lady Booby and Mrs. Slipslop, returns the reader to the vacillations of Lady Booby, now pouting. By this time, Mrs. Slipslop is also piqued at Joseph and vilifies his character, even claiming that Betty, the chambermaid, is with child by him. Lady Booby orders Slipslop to discharge them both and Slipslop, realizing that she has gone too far, tries to backtrack—but it is too late. Yet Lady Booby, warmed by the same passion for Joseph as is Slipslop, countermands her orders several times. Finally she resolves to see Joseph and to insult him before discarding him. This chapter closes with a wry apostrophe from Fielding to love's deceiving power of metamorphosis.

Fielding describes Joseph's physical charms and comments that this description might induce all ladies to "bridle their rampant passion for chastity." Continuing with his story,

Fielding shows us Lady Booby, seemingly scolding Joseph for his conduct, then embarking on another attempt at seduction, but utterly confounded by Joseph's sense of virtue. A reference by Joseph to the chastity of his sister, Pamela, completely undoes Lady Booby. She then dismisses Joseph from her household and, more mortified than ever, rings violently for Slipslop—who has been listening at the keyhole.

Lady Booby instructs Slipslop to see that Joseph is paid off and dismissed, but Slipslop is surprisingly pert in her replies. After a verbal parrying by the ladies, Slipslop remarks: "I know what I know," and Lady Booby realizes that her reputation now lies with Slipslop, whom she has just dismissed as well. She tells her steward, Mr. Peter Pounce, to turn Joseph out of the house that evening, but recalls Slipslop to see if she can patch things over. She quickly achieves a reconciliation with Slipslop, but the fact that her reputation is now in the hands of this gossipy servant tortures Lady Booby. Even more disturbing is the maelstrom of emotions concerning Joseph.

Joseph now understands the full drift of his mistress and unburdens himself in another letter to his sister. He is then called downstairs to receive the small remainder of his wages from the dishonest Peter Pounce. Stripped of his livery, he borrows a frock and breeches from one of the servants and leaves the house. Although it is seven o'clock in the evening, the moon is full, so Joseph resolves to begin his journey back to the country immediately.

Commentary

The mock-heroic description of the amorous Mrs. Slipslop as a "hungry tigress" is an excellent example of Fielding's use of the burlesque in his diction. The larger context of the pursuit of Joseph, however, offers ample illustration of the 'only source of the true Ridiculous'—affectation. The affectation of Lady Booby is more dangerous than Slipslop's because it involves deceit and hypocrisy. The hint to this is given by her casual— though outwardly correct—behavior after the death of Sir

Thomas. Resting on the seventh day from her mourning — or from her cards — she calls for Joseph, and falsely attributes his lack of forwardness to secrecy and designing modesty; she judges Joseph's actions by her own. In a series of leading questions, Lady Booby sounds out Joseph, but just as the simple Parson Adams failed to understand the affected language of Slipslop, so the straightforward Joseph fails to understand the innuendos of Lady Booby, who characteristically interprets his innocence as pretense.

The danger of Lady Booby's behavior lies in the turbulence of the conflict between passion and reason; she knows neither herself nor the true nature of Joseph, nor can she put into practice the principle of self-control. Joseph's tempting virginity still festers in her and we are thus prepared for her even more extravagant vacillations in Book IV. Her jealousy of Betty, the chambermaid, also suggests the jealousy she is to feel when she learns about Fanny. The mortification which Lady Booby feels at the revelation of Joseph's unshakable virtue is a result of her vanity. Above all, she is concerned for her reputation; she desperately wants Joseph but only if their affair can be kept secret. Her tremendous hypocrisy is exactly what Fielding most scorns. To illustrate this, he has mockingly inverted the situation of Richardson's *Pamela;* here it is the women who are sexually rampant.

If there is danger in Lady Booby's deceit, there is nothing more than ostentation in the open pursuit of Joseph by Mrs. Slipslop. Her vanity complements the hypocrisy of Lady Booby and, between the two of them, we have a perfect spectacle of affectation, the source of the true ridiculous. It is ludicrous that such a grotesque cripple as Slipslop should be casting eyes of affection on Joseph. The comedy is emphasized by Slipslop's manner of speaking; just as she thinks herself eminently suited for the handsome Joseph, so she considers her language learned and refined. In reality, her affected speech limps as brokenly as her ugly frame.

Between these two women, Fielding places the unassailable virtue of Joseph, who lives up to his biblical namesake, the proverbial master of chastity. The change from "Joey" to "Joseph" emphasizes the link. In a book concerned with the discrepancy between appearance and reality, Joseph, like Adams, reveals none at all between his honest face and his honest nature.

The confrontations are worthy of a playwright, and Fielding brings out the full dramatic effect of this particular triangle in its several permutations. He even draws attention to this himself, with such insertions as his remarks on love, and the reference to the arguments in Westminster reminds one of the author's presence.

The two letters which Joseph writes to his sister represent one of the novel's last links with Richardson's *Pamela.* Already *Joseph Andrews* is developing major themes of its own. In this section, the honesty, self-control, and chastity of Joseph predominate, but the theme of true charity emerges in the contrast between the greedy Peter Pounce, who strips Joseph of his livery, and the generous servant who provides Joseph with a frock and breeches. Later acts of charity often center on the metaphor and parable of clothing the naked and needy person.

As Joseph leaves London, "a bad place, [where] there is so little good fellowship, that the next-door neighbours don't know one another," the epic journey toward the Booby country seat and Joseph's self-knowledge begins in earnest.

Chapters 11-12

Summary

The moonlight was not Joseph's only inducement to set out immediately for Lady Booby's country seat. Living on a farm in the parish is Fanny Goodwill, whom Joseph has known and loved "from their infancy." Taking Parson Adams' advice, they have not married, waiting rather for the added wisdom of a few years' work and thrift. During Joseph's year of absence, the pair have not communicated, but have trusted in each other's fidelity and in the prospect of their future happiness.

Joseph is forced by a hailstorm to take shelter in an inn belonging to a man "called Plain Tim." When the storm is over, Joseph continues on his way with another traveller who was also stopped by the hail. After yet another halt, Joseph continues on his own, but is stripped, robbed, beaten unconscious, and thrown into a ditch by two thieves. A stagecoach comes up and after much argument amongst the selfish travellers, Joseph is lent a coat and lifted into the coach. The shallowness of the travellers is further emphasized when the coach is stopped by the thieves, but when they eventually reach an inn, Joseph is met with true kindness from a maid, who seats him by the fire while she makes up a bed for him. She tries to hasten along the surgeon, who promptly returns to bed when he hears that the injured person is a mere "foot-passenger." The master of the inn, Mr. Towwouse, sends a shirt to Joseph and is roundly abused by Mrs. Tow-wouse for doing so. The surgeon at last visits Joseph, and matters are not improved in the Tow-wouse household by his report that Joseph is in danger of his life.

Commentary

Many times throughout the book, Joseph is inspired by the sermons of Parson Adams. The parson's injunction of restraint to the lovers (and he is even more adamant in Book IV) reminds one of Prospero's motives concerning Ferdinand and Miranda in *The Tempest.* Yet Fielding does not really condemn warmth, whether it is in the love of Joseph and Fanny or the chance entanglement of Tow-wouse and Betty; like Prospero, he advocates not coldness but control.

The stagecoach episode recalls the parable of the Good Samaritan and underscores Fielding's theme of charity. While Joseph shows concern for the clothes he has borrowed, only one of the travellers displays any real compassion for Joseph's naked and battered state. The coachman thinks of his schedule and his fare, the lady affects shock at the thought of a naked man, the old gentleman wants to make haste to avoid being robbed himself, and the lawyer is worried only by the possible legal repercussions. These are all types of selfishness and ingratitude. Only the postillion feels truly compassionate: "he would rather ride in his shirt all his life than suffer a fellow-creature to lie in so miserable a condition." Fielding's aside that this man was later transported is his way of commenting on a society which would so harshly condemn a chicken thief. The other travellers are selfish and hypocritical and when the stagecoach is robbed, Fielding satirizes the lady who carries Nantes in her water bottle and the lawyer who is brave *after* the event. This foreshadows the case of the man who is brave *before* the event (Book II, Chapter 9); on that occasion, it is Adams who is truly brave, just as in this episode Joseph knocks down one of the robbers while being attacked from behind himself. Despite the barbed portrayal of hypocrisy in this section, one remembers Fielding's qualification in the preface: "the vices to be found here are rather the accidental consequences of some human frailty or foible." Indeed, the whole spirit of this passage is farcical. Some of Swift's vituperative descriptions of lawyers in *Gulliver's Travels* offer an interesting contrast. Where Swift is disgusted with basic human flaws, Fielding satirizes "accidental causes" rather than "causes habitually existing in the mind."

Amidst this imperfection, Joseph finds warmth and humanity. Neither Betty, the maid (is it merely coincidence that she bears the same name as the maid dismissed by Lady Booby?), nor Mr. Tow-wouse are perfect creatures, but their kindness to Joseph contrasts strongly with the behavior of the surgeon and with Mrs. Tow-wouse's outrage: "Common charity teaches us to provide for ourselves and our families; and I and mine won't be ruined by your charity, I assure you." Mrs. Tow-wouse's tavern is aptly named "The Dragon Inn." This and the collection of hypocrites who come to the inn contrast with the sign of the lion, "that magnanimous beast," found on the inn of the honest *plain* Tim. The theme of charity and good nature in relation to the selfish economics of everyday life is one that Fielding continues throughout *Joseph Andrews*.

Chapter 13

Summary

The surgeon despairs of Joseph's recovery, so Mr. Towwouse sends for a clergyman, Mr. Barnabas, who first drinks a dish of tea with the landlady and then a bowl of punch with the landlord before going up to see Joseph. Joseph is incoherent; he talks to himself about Fanny, but resigns himself without regret to the divine will. Barnabas considers all this "a rhapsody of nonsense." Later, when he finally talks with Joseph, his "Christian" admonitions to forget all carnal affections (Fanny) and to forgive everyone (the thieves) sound rather hollow. Barnabas descends for more punch while the good-natured Betty brings Joseph some tea (which Mrs. Tow-wouse had refused to serve him).

Commentary

Mr. Barnabas is one of the many hypocritical clergymen who are a disgrace to the cloth in a way that Adams, dishevelled on the outside but always decent on the inside, is not. The link between good nature and occupation is important; disposition demands practical exercise and encouragement. Hence Adams' office as a clergyman is important because "no other office could have given him so many opportunities of displaying his worthy inclinations" (Fielding's preface). Similarly, the hypocrites dissembling in the cloth can do great harm; there are no fewer than six such clergymen in *Joseph Andrews*, of whom Barnabas and Trulliber are the most glaring examples. Barnabas is more interested in punch than in his duties and he knows only the formulae of his faith. His dealings with Joseph are not at all related to Joseph's experience, and this discrepancy between formulae and "good works" (action) is one to which Fielding returns throughout the novel. The good nature of Joseph is, however, like Fielding's, essentially pragmatic; perhaps only Christ could forgive such enemies as Joseph encounters.

Again it is Betty who reveals a truly charitable heart in bringing Joseph the tea which was too much trouble for Mrs. Tow-wouse to prepare.

Chapters 14-15

Summary

Evening falls, and "a grave person" arrives at the inn. On hearing what has happened to Joseph—whose identity he does not yet know—he is immediately concerned for Joseph's health and safety amongst such uncharitable people. He inquires of the surgeon, who would rather talk in medical jargon than communicate. But the surgeon is interrupted—one of the thieves has been taken and, to the great joy of Joseph, a little piece of broken gold—a memento of Fanny—is found on him; the bundle of clothes stripped from Joseph is found shortly afterwards. The livery is recognized by the "grave" gentleman, who turns out to be none other than Parson Adams. Meanwhile, the mob that has gathered searches the captive, and the surgeon and Barnabas enter into a dispute as to which parties have the best legal claim to the recovered articles. The prisoner almost gains his freedom by continually protesting his innocence, but Betty reminds the company of the evidence of the piece of gold, and the prisoner is secured for the night.

Betty tells her mistress that she believes Joseph to be "a greater man than they took him for," as he seems to be on intimate terms with Parson Adams; Mrs. Tow-wouse immediately changes her attitude. Adams tells Joseph that he is on his way to London to publish three volumes of sermons, but insists on staying with Joseph and offers him the contents of his pockets—less than ten shillings. Joseph is overcome with gratitude; fortunately, he is in better shape than the opportunist surgeon will admit.

The next morning, Barnabas and the surgeon return to see the thief conveyed before the justice. They have spent the night arguing over legal procedures, and Fielding concludes the chapter with an apostrophe to vanity to underscore their behavior—and to "lengthen out a short chapter."

Commentary

Adams soon perceives that hunger is Joseph's most pressing ailment, and it is the gibberish of the surgeon which is the real example of "a rhapsody of nonsense." In legal and other matters, both Barnabas and the surgeon are motivated by vanity rather than by any sense of duty; their concern is for the advertisement of their own assumed abilities rather than for public justice. Contrasted to this pretence is Adams' "perfect simplicity," hinted at by the fact that all he knows comes from books; Adams is serious and simple—but sincere. His immediate concern for the plight of the footman, whom he does not know at first to be Joseph, testifies to this. He is willing to delay a journey which is important to him and his family, and his offer to give his entire "fortune" of less than ten shillings to Joseph contrasts with the selfish change in the attitude of Mrs. Tow-wouse. Where Adams' sympathies are truly Christian, Mrs. Tow-wouse considers a person worthy of Christian compassion to be the opposite of a vagabond; in other words, a Christian is someone who is likely to be able to pay his bill.

Fielding continues to amplify his theme of getting to the heart of true good nature and, in his concluding remarks on vanity, stresses the difficulty of penetrating the disguises which vanity tempts people to assume. His tone mocks even himself, for far from being carried away by his own indignation, with his several paragraphs deploring vanity, he confesses that he is really only lengthening out his chapter.

Chapter 16

Summary

The vain ostentation of Barnabas and the surgeon is in contrast to the thief, who, the pair of legal wranglers find on their return, has escaped — thanks to the carelessness — or dishonesty — of the constable, Tom Suckbribe.

Adams realizes that as Joseph is not yet well enough to travel that day he will require more money. He takes Tow-wouse aside and asks him for three guineas, at the same time offering him what he thinks is ample security. But the security turns out to be the sermons, and so Tow-wouse hurries off with a "Coming, sir," to no one in particular.

While Adams takes comfort in his pipe, a coach and six arrive at the inn, and the coachman and his master engage in a facetious slanging match. Barnabas discovers through one of the footmen of this coach that Adams is a clergyman, and over a bowl of punch, they discuss Adams' volumes of sermons. Barnabas has had no success with his own and casts doubt on the prospect of Adams making any money by publishing his.

Joseph is now almost fully recovered, and Adams and he agree to part on their separate ways, Adams to London and Joseph to the Booby country-seat. Joseph retires to his chamber while Adams goes down to meet a friend of Mr. Barnabas who has just arrived at the inn.

Commentary

The constable's name, Tom Suckbribe, indicates that the thief owes his escape to more than the constable's negligence. Many of the names (Whipwell, Slipslop, Booby, Peter Pounce, Fanny Goodwill, Mrs. Grave-airs, etc.) carry on the Jonsonian tradition of humors, and Fielding himself emphasizes in the first chapter of Book III that his characters are types.

Mrs. Tow-wouse is as concerned with money as is Tom Suckbribe, and her expostulation of "feeling" is an ironic inversion of real values: "you have no more feeling than a deal board. If a man lived a fortnight in your house without spending a penny, you would never put him in mind of it." Parson Adams, on the other hand, who generously offers Joseph his few shillings, is completely naive about the economics of everyday life; it is not surprising that he fails to convince Mr. Tow-wouse of the worth of his sermons in terms of hard cash. Again the actual is juxtaposed to a better form of conduct. In everyday life, the province of the novel, we must scrabble like the Tow-wouses — but for all its intangibility is not the good nature of Adams just as important and real? In any case, there is already a hint in Adams' reference to Tillotson's sermons that good nature must be translated into action. Neither Adams' sermons, which serve as an ideal to Joseph, nor the good actions of such people as Betty and the postillion may be acceptable to society, but they are nevertheless an important part of human conduct. Clearly there is more in a novel than a mere account of life as it *is*. In *Joseph Andrews*, the values are certainly possible if not practical.

The small incident of the facetious dialogue between the coachman and his master is an example of Fielding's digressions that elsewhere are expanded on a larger scale. In fact, such digressions as this conversation and the history of Leonora in Book II link circles. The theme of these diversions — here, the casual betting between roguish "friends" contrasts with the real concern over money shown by Adams on Joseph's behalf — are miniature views of the concern of this novel.

Chapters 17-18

Summary

Much to Adams' delight, the friend of Barnabas proves to be a bookseller, to whom he proceeds to offer his sermons. The bookseller, who says that he dislikes sermons only because they don't sell, adds that he will take them to London with him. A discussion develops between Adams and Barnabas over the Methodist doctrines of George Whitefield. Barnabas reviles Whitefield because he advocates continual preaching and praying for clergymen rather than more pleasurable pursuits, while Adams, though agreeing with Whitefield that the business of clergymen should not be with things which savor strongly of this world, strongly criticizes the "detestable doctrine of faith against good works." On hearing that Adams' sermons inculcate the opposite opinion, that virtuous heathens are more acceptable to God than are vicious Christians, the bookseller immediately backtracks, saying that he will take on no book which the clergy would be certain to denounce. Talking of the restoration of the true use of Christianity, Adams mentions a book which sets Barnabas to spluttering, though he has read not one syllable of it.

Their altercation is interrupted by an uproar in the inn. Mrs. Tow-wouse has caught her husband making love to Betty, the chambermaid, and the two women are at loggerheads. Mrs. Tow-wouse arms herself with the kitchen spit, but is restrained by Mr. Adams.

Betty, though generous and compassionate, has a constitution "composed of those warm ingredients which, though the purity of courts or nunneries might have happily controlled them, were by no means able to endure the ticklish situation of a chambermaid at an inn." Heretofore, she has succumbed to the amorous advances of many, though not to those of Mr. Tow-wouse, who has long languished for her. She conceives a passion for Joseph, which on this occasion reached such a height that the modest Joseph was forced to shut her out of his room; but, on retiring to make Mr. Tow-wouse's bed, she came across Mr. Tow-wouse himself and in her heightened state of passion, she submitted to his will. At this point, Mrs. Tow-wouse entered the bedroom. Betty is dismissed, and Mrs. Tow-wouse hangs the albatross of adultery round her husband's neck for the remainder of his life.

Commentary

Adams again reveals his simplicity in financial matters. He explains his impoverished state in all honesty to the bookseller, completely undermining his own bargaining position. But the commercial world is not the one in which Adams lives; he states that an honest mind would rather lose money by conveying good instructions to mankind than gain by propagating evil. Adams' real concerns emerge in his comments on the Methodist doctrine which puts faith before good works. Adams considers that nothing can have a more pernicious influence on society than last-minute repentance; active virtue is always more important than faith.

This again bears on how the novel "rectifies" real life. Were the results of Adams' ecstatic moments confined to smoking a pipe, snapping his fingers, and taking a turn or two about the room, one might argue that he lives on a quite separate plane. But the strength with which he restrains Mrs. Tow-wouse is part of Adams' own doctrine of good works, to be fully implemented in the present.

The same theme emerges in Fielding's tolerant treatment of Betty and Mr. Tow-wouse. Fielding proposes more realistic alternatives to vice. "I have done nothing that's unnatural," Betty exclaims, and the violence of Mr. Tow-wouse's passion, "like water, which is stopt from its usual current in one place . . . *naturally* sought a vent in another." Even when describing the venereal disease, Fielding's tone is light as he puns that Betty's charms set soldiers and squires afire in more ways than one. The strong effect of environment on both Betty and Mr. Tow-wouse again indicates Fielding's concern with the possibility of implementing higher standards in the here and now. Inclination and environment bear upon one another closely.

Fielding's comments on Joseph's chastity in the face of Betty's passionate embrace soar to the level of the mock-heroic and there is no concern on Fielding's part that Betty's passions are sated by the first man who comes along. The behavior of Betty and Mr. Tow-wouse reminds the reader not to take Joseph's rigid chastity too seriously. Their lapse is not wholly condoned, but Fielding's tone emphasizes that Betty's good nature and compassion are more important than prudish hypocrisy.

BOOK II

Chapter 1

Summary and Commentary

Fielding briefly justifies his division of *Joseph Andrews* into sections or "books." He refers wryly to the sanction provided by Homer and Virgil, who divided their epics into "books." Moreover, he says, modern authors can make more money by publishing piecemeal. Fielding stresses that, by dividing his novel into separate books, his readers are afforded a sort of "inn or resting-place" for contemplating what they have just read. As readers of a novel organized by one "initiated into the science of authoring," we need time to take stock of the patterns that have been developing. Only by doing this will we fully understand some "curious productions of nature"; in effect, Fielding helps us get at the "meat" of this work by "carving" it for us.

Chapters 2-3

Summary

Joseph and Adams are about to go on their separate ways when it is discovered that Adams has nothing more in his saddle bags than his clothes, which his practical wife thought would be more useful to him than his sermons. Adams now has no reason for going to London and says he is just as happy to travel back to the Booby country-seat with Joseph. The pair of them set out "to ride and tie," Adams departing on foot, Joseph to go ahead, for a while, on horseback. The parson starts off, but before Joseph can leave, he is presented with a bill: Adams forgot to settle up for the horse. Joseph has but sixpence and the little piece of gold which is a memento of Fanny; on seeing the gold, the avaricious Mrs. Tow-wouse refuses to give him credit. Meanwhile, Adams is concerned that there is no sign of Joseph, so, having waded unnecessarily through some flood water he sits down to read in his copy of Aeschylus, failing to notice that there is an inn not more than a stone's throw away. A horseman, however, directs him to it and he has no more than seated himself when two men enter and refer to Joseph's predicament. While drinking with the man, Adams asks about the owner of a house he passed, and the two men launch into entirely different accounts of the owner; one vilifies his character while the other praises him. The storm ceases and, after the two travelers have left, the puzzled Adams asks the innkeeper to resolve the contradiction. It appears that the gentleman in question, a justice, has decided only one case recently—in which these two men were the opposing parties. Adams is astonished by the lies they have told and admonishes his host never to lie, for the sake of his immortal soul. "What signifies talking about matters so far off?" replies the down-to-earth host, and goes off to draw some more beer. Just then a coach approaches. It happens that one of the women in it has redeemed Joseph and also Adams' horse; to his surprise, Adams discovers that it is none other than Mrs. Slipslop. Joseph arrives and, as they all set off—Adams in the coach, Joseph on the horse—Adams discusses Lady Booby's recent behavior. He finds that Slipslop's criticism of her mistress and pat flattery of the late Sir Thomas are curious reversals of her former opinions. At this point, one of the ladies in the coach draws their attention to a mansion they are passing; it is, she says, the home of "the unfortunate Leonora." Having whetted the curiosity of her fellow-travellers, she begins the history of Leonora.

Commentary

The events of these two chapters emphasize some of the salient points of the character of Parson Adams. In Chapter 2, his forgetfulness is apparent many times. He has left his sermons at home and is so absent-minded as to not compute that nine volumes of sermons could never have fit into his saddle bags anyway. He forgets to pay for the care of his horse, and drenches himself because he sees only what is immediately in front of him—though not what is only a stone's throw away. Even in all this humorous muddle, however, there are several small points which prepare us for some important positive qualities in Chapter 3. Adams philosophically accepts the disappointment of the missing sermons and, in his confrontation with the flood water, he is certainly direct. As for the horse, it has been well looked after because Adams borrowed the animal from his clerk; one remembers the concern shown by Joseph for the borrowed clothes in Book I, Chapter 12. If Adams is more interested in the abstract world of Aeschylus than in the way to an alehouse, Joseph is a kindred spirit. To Mrs. Tow-Wouse, gold is money; to Joseph the bit of broken gold is a symbol and a reminder of his beloved Fanny.

The argument between the two men in the alehouse is an encapsulated incident which prefigures the lengthier Leonora digression. It illustrates well one of the recurring themes of *Joseph Andrews*; the way in which self-interest clouds the truth. When Adams hears the reasons for the false summaries of the justice's character, his reaction is immediate and heartfelt: "out of love to yourself, you should confine yourself to truth." Such self-interest is hardly of this world, and the earnestness of Adams is comic. The practical host wins a sympathetic smile from us, just as we give an amused nod to Harry Bailey, the host who makes the most of Chaucer's Canterbury pilgrims. The theme of getting past appearance and discovering truth is continued with the arrival of Mrs. Slipslop. The hostess fails to link her inquiries after a clergyman with the extraordinary appearance of Adams, whom she mistakes for a peddler travelling to a fair. And the vacillations in Mrs. Slipslop's estimation of Lady Booby and her late husband are an echo of the false appraisals given by the two travellers. These parallel instances of deceptive appearances prepare us for the tale of Leonora.

Chapter 4

Summary

Leonora, eighteen years old, was the daughter of a gentleman of fortune and now lived with an aunt. Vivacious and vain, she rarely missed a ball or other public meeting and had singled out a young gentleman, Horatio, from her many admirers at these gatherings. Horatio, handsome and dignified, eventually brought himself to ask for her hand, and Leonora accepted. The lady recounting the tale then recites from memory an exchange of letters in which the tenderest affections are expressed; indeed, everything was in "such great forwardness" that the wedding date was fixed and was now but a fortnight away. At this time, Horatio, who was a barrister, went off to the county sessions; meanwhile, Leonora, at home, spied a coach and six passing by her window and declared: "O, I am in love with that equipage!" Bellarmine, the owner of the coach and six and lately arrived from Paris, arrived in all his French finery at an assembly held that evening. He was immediately impressed by Leonora's beauty. As for Leonora, she had earlier decided not to dance in Horatio's absence. But her head was quite turned by the handsome and wealthy Bellarmine, and she danced with him the whole night. The next afternoon Bellarmine proposed to Leonora. Thoughts of Horatio worried at her conscience for a little while, but her aunt soon put a stop to her vacillations: "I assure you there is not anything worth our regard besides money." That evening Leonora and Bellarmine were at dinner, and Bellarmine was holding forth about his fancy clothes when—without warning—Horatio entered. To his utter surprise, he found himself treated by Leonora as no more than a "common acquaintance," while Bellarmine hummed an opera tune and strolled around the room in a minuet step. Leonora upbraided Horatio, only to discover that her "protector" quickly wilted before the real courage of Horatio. The aunt entered then and appraised Horatio of the true state of affairs, whereupon he demanded satisfaction from Bellarmine. This was temporarily forestalled by the ladies, but Leonora awakened next morning to the dismal news that Bellarmine had been mortally wounded by Horatio. While Leonora assumed various frantic poses of grief, her aunt prudently advised her to make up with Horatio, but this only caused a bout of recrimination between the two ladies. A letter arrived shortly from Bellarmine; there was nothing mortal about his wound. Leonora's remorse immediately vanished, and she resolved to visit Bellarmine despite her aunt's advice not to overplay her hand. Just at that moment, the coach—much to the disappointment of the insatiably curious Adams—arrives at an inn.

Chapter 5

Summary

Joseph is already at the inn, sitting in the kitchen and suffering from a heavy fall from Adams' eccentric horse. The hostess, who is treating the contusion, is berated by her husband for wasting time on a mere footman — to which Adams replies that he believes the devil has more humanity. This sparks off a fistfight in which Adams lays out the host, then promptly receives from the hostess a panful of hog's blood in the face. Mrs. Slipslop enters and, seeing Adams dripping with blood, seizes the hostess, whose anguished cries bring the rest of the company into the room. One of the two men who had earlier quarrelled over the character of the justice (see Chapter 3) advises the host to recover damages against Adams; "I must speak the truth," he says, and offers his own distorted views as evidence. The host has no faith in the law, however, and turns on his wife for wasting his hog's puddings. Meanwhile, the other gentleman encourages Parson Adams to take out a suit against the host, but Adams admits that it was he who struck the first blow and is horrified by the gentleman's suggestion that Joseph, as the only witness, should lie in Adams' behalf.

The quarrel is finally settled, and the coachman is anxious to be on his way. Mrs. Grave-airs, however, refuses to admit a mere footman (Joseph) into the coach. This occasions an altercation between her and Mrs. Slipslop, which is ended only by the arrival of Mrs. Grave-air's father, who takes his daughter away with him. Once in the coach, the women begin berating the character of Mrs. Grave-airs. Mrs. Slipslop, "not a cup too low," entertains notions of playing the good Christian to Joseph and is suspiciously affectionate. To prevent any improper consequences, one of the ladies begs for the story of Leonora to be resumed.

Commentary

The surly behavior of the host is based on his false interpretation of appearance; in his view, Joseph does not merit any attention because he wears the livery of a footman; and Adams, in his usual dishevelled state, merits only scorn. Condemning the host, Fielding once again shows that he champions an active sense of humanity, and in the hostess's care for Joseph, there may even be an echo of Martha's washing the feet of Jesus. Like Betty, the hostess is no model of perfection, but we admire her for her charity and even for her loyalty to her husband. Once again, there is no priggishness in Adams; he preaches here as a pugilist, pointing up the importance of an active virtue. His values are untainted by experience, which, like the hog's blood, washes off him. In contrast to Adams is the devious behavior of the two gentlemen, both ready to falsify evidence to suit themselves. It is special "interest" too which gives Mrs. Slipslop a short-lived cause for worry. Her vanity led her to match herself against Mrs. Grave-airs, and when she discovers this lady's connections, she fears she may have gone too far—until she remembers the hold she has over Lady Booby. The traveller with the affected and distorted smattering of Italian underscores the vanity and affectation of both Mrs. Grave-airs and Mrs. Slipslop, whose memory of her mistress' sexual advances toward Joseph is, in turn, thrown into an ironic light by her own compulsion for Joseph, who, as she says, would warm any Christian woman's blood.

Chapter 5 provides an interlude in Fielding's long digression about Leonora. It is an insertion of scrappiness, of real life, placed midway in a polished and well-turned tale; in a sense, Chapters 4, 5, and 6 are a microcosm of *Joseph Andrews* itself.

Chapter 6

Summary

Leonora's unceasing attention to the wounded Bellarmine occasioned some malicious gossip amongst the ladies of the town. But when Bellarmine was recovered, he set out to discuss the terms of his marriage to Leonora with her father, a callous man who looked on his children as rivals in the enjoyment of his own ruthlessly amassed fortune. The match with Bellarmine at first seemed to the father as most advantageous, but when Bellarmine mentioned the matter of a dowry, the father shied away, berating the extravagance of the youth of the age. Bellarmine vainly tried to hold him to the subject of a dowry, finally stating that he could not marry Leonora without one. Leonora's father refused to advance so much as a shilling, and within a few days, Leonora received a letter from Bellarmine, now returned to Paris, in which she learned that he was not the "heureux person destined for [her] divine arms." Completely distraught, Leonora retired to the house seen earlier from the coach. Today, Horatio prospers, but he is still single and never hears the name of Leonora without a sigh.

Commentary

At first, the story of Leonora would appear to be an isolated narrative pocket which is only barely related to the rest of the novel. Its main concern, however, is central to *Joseph Andrews* and is expressed in a by-now-familiar metaphor; that is, what lies behind a person's clothes and appearance? Horatio, though living up to the dignity apparent in his own bearing, is deceived by the sprightliness in Leonora's countenance, while Leonora manufactured all manner of passion on the strength of Bellarmine's French affectations. The cause of this passion, which "distorted her person into several shapes, and her face into several laughs, without any reason," is vanity, one of the sources of the affectation which Fielding satirizes throughout the novel. Leonora is linked to Lady Booby, not only because she is vain, but by the way in which hypocrisy and passion control her sensibilities. Her passion is encouraged by the avaricious "reason" of her aunt, whose definition of love is synonymous with self-interest. How different is the aunt's concern for young love when compared with the heartfelt concern of Parson Adams for Joseph and Fanny.

Confronted by Horatio, Leonora concerned herself with the "ceremonies of good breeding"; Horatio, however, was made of sterner stuff and, like Adams, goes to the heart of the matter with physical courage. "The seat of valor is not in the countenance," Fielding comments, and it is only just that the cowardly Bellarmine should be a victim of the *active* virtue of Horatio. During the remainder of the tale, the themes of affectation and self-interest are continued. Leonora's aunt continued to advise her niece to be more reserved toward Bellarmine, but Leonora irretrievably attached herself to Bellarmine — and, as a consequence, she was censured by the town ladies, especially by Lindamira, whose name, in Spanish, means the same as Bellarmine's in French: beautiful face. Despite all the affectations of love, passion, and devotion, Bellarmine's interest in Leonora was purely financial. But Leonora's father — who had the reputation of being a good parent — loved his gold better than his daughter. Ironically, it was only Horatio who eventually made money — and, to him, it was the memory of Leonora that mattered most.

Chapters 7-9

Summary

The coach now catches up with Adams, who is so pleased at getting Joseph into the coach that he has quite forgotten to redeem the horse from the stable. Despite the efforts of the coach to overtake him, Adams scampers ahead and soon manages to miss his way. Resting on the summit of a hill, he pulls out his copy of Aeschylus, but is startled by a gunshot; soon the sportsman, at first suspicious of Adams' dishevelled appearance, starts to talk to him, complaining that the soldiers quartered nearby have killed all the game. If only they were as accurate with the enemy, the man complains. Then he launches into praise for a man who is willing to lay down his life for his country. Adams rebukes his companion's swearing, but commends his sentiment, and engages on a dissertation of his own. In this, he relates how in various elections his vote and influence over his nephew, an alderman of a corporation, have been sought after by fickle politicians, culminating with Sir Thomas Booby who, for all his apparent good intentions, failed like the others to reward Adams with the living he had promised him — perhaps because Lady Booby did not think his clothes "good enough for the gentry at her table." Now that his nephew is dead, Adams no longer considers himself such a political wedge, but he has continued to put a dash or two of politics into his sermons, hoping that Sir Thomas might eventually procure an ordination for his thirty-year-old son, in whom Adams has inculcated his own principles of serving God and Country. The gentleman then launches forth on his theme of bravery once again, telling Adams that he has disinherited a nephew whom he believed to be dragging his feet, with regard to active service; Adams advises a more forgiving attitude.

Adams sees that the stagecoach is now three miles ahead of him, but the gentleman persuades him not to try and catch up with the coach so late in the evening, and offers him accommodations at his house. On their way there, the gentleman continues to praise bravery, but, when they hear a woman shrieking for help, this same gentleman runs to the safety of his house, while Adams, snapping his fingers, makes for the fray and finds a woman being assaulted. Adams promptly cracks his crabstick on the fellow's head, but the thick-skulled assailant manages to give Adams a drubbing before the parson finally lays him out with a solid clip to the chin—so solid indeed that Adams fears he has killed the man. The woman explains to Adams how she had been travelling to London and had fallen in with this man for company, only to find that his intentions went far beyond those of a mere travelling-companion. Adams thanks Providence for sending him to the rescue in time and—if the fellow is indeed dead—Adams relies on the goodness of his intention to excuse him in the next world and on the woman's evidence to acquit him in this.

Commentary

Adams may lose his way in the most short-sighted manner, but we already know that his innocence has a surer foundation of virtue than that suggested by the bluster of the sportsman. Both his virtue and his innocence are apparent in the account he gives of his unfortunate brushes with political matters, occasioned by the importance of his nephew. He stands by his word in all good faith whatever the temptation, yet is consistently surprised that those he supports always fail to fulfill their promises to him. Nevertheless, he interprets the failings of such men as Sir Oliver Hearty and Sir Thomas Booby in the most charitable light, and there is justification as well as innocence—and a touch of vanity—in the hope that if his son is ever "of as much consequence in a public light as his father once was," he will use his talents as honestly.

Such names as Colonel Courtly and Esquire Fickle are part of Fielding's satire, and this account may well refer to Fielding's own experience when he broke his long-standing association with *The Champion* and his opposition to Walpole. In their race for power (which they gained in February, 1742), the opposition—the Patriots—forgot their obligations to such allies as Fielding, who consequently broke with them despite his need for money. The sportsman's patriotic protestations of valor on behalf of his country prove to be as empty as the principles and promises of the actual so-called Patriots.

In contrast to the rapid retreat of the sportsman, we are presented with Adams' example of bravery; appearances have again proved to be deceptive. In his mocking comments about the thickness of the ravisher's head (comments which extend to the commanders of armies and empires), Fielding is again discrediting those whom we traditionally regard as heroes so that he can highlight the real heroism of Adams, who, regretting the death—so he thinks—of his opponent, nonetheless says: "but God's will be done." Virtue, come what may, must always be put into practice, according to Adams' code.

Chapters 10-11

Summary

A group of young "bird-batters" discovers the distraught woman and her rescuer; Adams is still vacillating between faith in his legs or in the law. He tries to relate what has happened, but the canny villain interrupts with his own version: he is a poor traveller who was robbed by this pair of rogues! Catching a pair of thieves immediately seems better sport than catching birds, and so the bird-batters march Adams and the woman off to the justice. The resigned Adams, constantly sympathetic toward his companion, misses an opportunity to escape, for when the clerk of the company mentions the possibility of an 80 pound reward they all start to bicker about their share. In his mournful ejaculations, Adams mentions the name of Joseph Andrews, which leads to the revelation that the woman is none other than Joseph's beloved Fanny, who had heard of Joseph's misfortune, had immediately abandoned the cow she was milking, and set out to find Joseph. Fanny denies her passion to Adams, who "never saw farther into people than they desired to let him," but Fielding tells us that she loved Joseph "with inexpressible violence."

Adams and Fanny are put in a stable while the justice, just returned from a fox chase, finishes his dinner. Afterward, the justice, "being in the height of his mirth and his cups," proceeds to "have good sport" with them, without any regard to the issues at stake. While lewd remarks are leveled at Fanny, a witty fellow spies Adams' cassock beneath his greatcoat and taunts him with several lines of Latin. Adams quickly challenges the wit's linguistic mistakes — but, to the amusement of the crowd, he has no money to back up his wager. Meanwhile, the justice orders the clerk to make the *mittimus* (without reading a word of the depositions), and the indignant objections from Adams do nothing to prick his conscience. At this point, the clerk introduces into the evidence Adams' copy of Aeschylus, which is literally and figuratively Greek to the justice, who mutters darkly about "cyphers." The parson of the parish fares little better with the book, and the justice triumphantly takes Aeschylus to be Adams' fictitious name. By chance, a squire in the crowd recognizes Adams and, when the justice hears Adams referred to as a clergyman and gentleman, he hastily tries to make amends. Adams gives the true account of the whole affair, which the justice believes as readily as he did the first version. The villain of the episode, however, has quietly withdrawn, leaving the bird-batters in a loud drunken quarrel concerning who *would* have received the most money had Adams been convicted. Adams takes a drink with the justice and, despite his wise observations on the folly of people who argue vehemently about matters of small import to them, he almost comes to blows with the justice in a debate on the conduct of the arraignment. Fanny interrupts the dispute when she learns that a young fellow is about to set out for the inn where Joseph's stagecoach has stopped. She and Adams accompany the young man to the inn.

Commentary

Though Adams is accused of stealing his cassock, it is the ignorant parson of the parish who proves to be the impostor. The theme of incompetent clergymen is soon to be filled out by the ale-swilling Parson Trulliber. To provide spice to his satire, Fielding inserts a parody on "a knowledge of Latin" and also provides us with a justice, thick and bloated from his own meal. Fielding was himself a magistrate and had first-hand knowledge of the abuse of common law by those supposed to be on the right side of it. The world of Aeschylus, the feeder of Adams' better self, is unknown to these lesser mortals—but Fielding emphasizes Adams' humanity by allowing him, despite his own philosophical observations, to warm up almost to boiling point in his debate with the justice.

Chapters 12-13

Summary

A storm forces Adams and Fanny to take shelter in an alehouse and, while Adams tests the brew, Fielding gives the reader a portrait of Fanny. She is exquisite, and even her few minor blemishes do not mar the overall effect of her beauty; her most important feature, however, is her "natural gentility." Returning to the narrative, Fielding inserts several verses of a long ballad about unrequited love, sung by a sweet-voiced young man in another part of the alehouse. We guess who he is when Fanny faints at the close of the song. Adams leaps up, dropping his beloved copy of Aeschylus into the fire as he roars for help. At this, the unseen "nightingale" appears and proves to be none other than Joseph Andrews, who immediately sets about reviving Fanny with kisses. Adams skips for joy, the modest Fanny is embarrassed, and the jealous Mrs. Slipslop exits in a haughty sweep, completely ignoring Fanny's curtsy to her. This is a deliberate snub, and to explain Slipslop's behavior, Fielding explains his theory about the two classes into which people are divided—the high and the low. These are composed of the fashionable and the unfashionable, the latter pursuing and aping the former all the way up the social ladder, while the former disdain their "inferiors." Adams, who is ignorant of these intricacies of the social mechanism, follows Slipslop and tries to jog her memory about Fanny, whom Slipslop now deigns to barely remember. While Adams praises Fanny's chastity, Slipslop, in her jealous pique, upbraids him for his violence in rescuing Fanny and casts aspersions on Fanny's character. Outside, the storm is now over, but to Slipslop's chagrin, Joseph refuses to travel on without Fanny; for the second time that evening, a rape has been prevented!

While Adams dozes by the fire, Joseph and Fanny declare their love for each other. Enraptured, Joseph wakes Adams to ask him to marry them. Adams refuses, stressing the importance of publishing the banns; Joseph must contain himself a little longer.

The three of them prepare to set off, as it is now daylight, but the reckoning of seven shillings (because of Adams' thirst) causes a slight delay. Adams is suddenly struck by an idea and asks the hostess if there is a clergyman in the parish. Finding that there is, Adams joyfully leaves Fanny and Joseph, telling them that he has a "brother" in the parish who will pay the bill, and that he will return shortly with the money.

Commentary

It is clearly Fanny's inner worth that Fielding considers most important, and she responds to the warm-blooded Joseph (whose song is full of sexual innuendoes) with just the proper degree of shyness and modesty. Their reunion brings out the truly charitable nature of Adams, his joy at the happiness of *others*. In contrast to this, we have the affected snobbishness of Slipslop, whose jealous disdain of Fanny prefigures Lady Booby's behavior in Book IV. This imitation of "fashion" throughout the social scale provides Fielding with material for his lengthy digression; if the gods made men only to laugh at them, Fielding says, there is no other human characteristic which serves the purpose so well. Meanwhile, we chuckle kindly at Adams' insistence on the proper rites and forms for the wedding of Joseph and Fanny; also, as the chapter closes, we have the feeling that the parson's naïvete over money matters is about to get him into trouble once again.

Chapters 14-15

Summary

Adams arrives at the house of Parson Trulliber, who is more of a farmer than a clergyman, for his wife runs the dairy while he sees to the pigs, whom he resembles in size and nature. Trulliber thinks that Adams has come to buy some of his hogs, and receives him with such enthusiasm that the unfortunate Adams finds himself propelled into the pig sty to make a closer acquaintance with his prospective purchases. Thoroughly confused, Adams takes hold of a pig's tail; the pig leaps up and throws Adams down in the mire. *"Nihil habeo cum porcis,"* cries Adams, and Trulliber, amused by the incident, says that his wife is to blame for the misunderstanding. Once inside and cleaned up a bit, Adams reveals who he is and what he needs: money, a subject which exposes Trulliber's hypocrisy. Adams is no clergyman, but a vagabond, he roars, and, at the same time, berates his poor wife. When Adams calmly tells Trulliber that *he* is no Christian because he does not actively practice charity, Trulliber doubles up his fists. Adams is not provoked, however, and leaves with the remark that he is sorry to see such men in religious orders.

The parson returns penniless to Joseph and Fanny, but the hostess surprises them all by allowing them credit and wishing them a good journey. Her generosity, however, is not genuine;

she has misunderstood Joseph and believes Adams to be the *natural* brother of Trulliber, not merely his "brother in divinity." As they are about to leave, Adams remembers that he left his greatcoat and hat at Trulliber's house and, to Adams' relief, the hostess offers to fetch these for him. It is an unfortunate favor. Trulliber denounces Adams to the hostess in no uncertain terms and, on her return, she demands her money. To Adams' distress, a journey round the parish yields nothing, but chance enters our story: a fellow-traveller in the inn who has overheard the hostess' hard remarks takes Adams aside and asks him how much is owed. A loan is made and Adams, Fanny, and Joseph are saved by the goodness of a poor peddler. After telling the peddler where to call to be repaid, the travellers leave their sour-faced hostess and the sour-soul parish.

Commentary

The subject of these two chapters is true charity. Trulliber is a boor, the worst of the six incompetent parsons we meet in *Joseph Andrews*. His concerns are very much with this world; he has no feeling for his guest either as a man or as a fellow parson, he bullies his wife unmercifully, and—worst of all—he is entirely ignorant of the meaning of charity: "I know what charity is, better than to give to vagabonds." He rages to Adams about his appearance, commenting sarcastically upon his shabby cassock and his lack of a horse; for him the "dignity of the cloth has a literal meaning only. The nature of his hypocrisy links him to that other odious parson, Barnabas. Both men ignore the importance of good works; Trulliber, indeed, does nothing to help Adams, and his own attitude is echoed throughout his parish. One is reminded here of Adams' criticism of George Whitefield's "detestable doctrine of faith against good works" in Book I, Chapter 17. The hostess is dominated by the worldly patronage of Trulliber, and her hypocrisy has the stamp of her master; her comment that people should not pretend to be what they are not is as ironic as Trulliber's claim to know what charity is. It is only the poor peddler who knows the true nature of charity. As with the postillion who offers his greatcoat to the battered Joseph (Book I, Chapter 12), society has not been kind to this truly compassionate man.

The handling of Adams' confrontation with Trulliber shows Fielding's artistry at his best. There is, first of all, the warm humor of Adams' naïvete and unfortunate tumble into the mire, but this, like the hog's blood, will wash off him as all experience seems to do. The innocence of Adams is beautifully compounded into a classic reversal as Trulliber realizes that—far from being paid money—he is being asked for it. Fielding enters the narrative with half a dozen imagined examples of reversal to heighten this superbly dramatic moment. The playwright's eye is everywhere apparent—in the way in which Adams misunderstands the enraged and disillusioned Trulliber, in the sharp exchange of dialogue which follows this, and in such small gems as the wife dropping to her knees and begging Adams not to rob them! Indeed, Fielding's use of Trulliber's wife consistently lends an extra dimension to the conflict between Trulliber and Adams. The farcical tone is there too, both in the opening description of Trulliber and in the way Fielding unashamedly enters the narrative to manipulate events to a farcical conclusion.

Chapters 16-17

Summary

On the road again, the travellers meet a gentleman who appears to be all openness and magnanimity. He invites them to share some refreshment with him in the inn of the parish—where he owns a large mansion—and offers Adams the living of this particular parish upon the death of the present incumbent. In addition to other generous offers, the gentleman suggests that they avail themselves of his hospitality for a couple of days; Adams is overcome, but no sooner have Adams, Joseph and Fanny accepted than the gentleman suddenly "remembers" that his housekeeper is away. Next morning, he also finds himself unable to provide the horses he had promised; it is, he says, the groom's fault, and Adams is aghast at the way this good-natured gentleman is abused by his servants. Joseph is more concerned about how they are going to pay the bill for their night's lodging at the inn. They send a boy for the gentleman, who, it appears, has departed on a month's journey. The host confirms the suspicions that Joseph has entertained for some time about the sincerity of this gentleman. The host relates previous examples of the emptiness of this gentleman's promises and scoffs at Adams' remark about the sweetness of his countenance, for the travels of the host as a seafaring man have taught him never to trust a man's face. Adams, as usual, takes up the argument and claims to have travelled also, but it turns out that his travelling has been entirely in books, "the only way of travelling by which any knowledge is to be acquired." The host briskly retorts that experience is the best teacher, and extends his argument to defend the practice of trade, which, he claims, provides clothes, wine and other necessities of life. These to Adams are luxuries; the necessities are provided by the learning of the clergy, who clothe and feed people in a more valuable way. Fortunately for the peace of all, Joseph and Fanny, who have been conversing in the garden, interrupt the argument and the three renew their journey.

Commentary

Fielding continues to stress the themes of hypocrisy and true charity. Adams, eternally innocent, once again judges man at face value and is naively ecstatic at the hollow offers of the gentleman, believing his charity to be "of the true primitive kind." It is a sign of Joseph's increasing maturity that his estimation of the gentleman is more acute; his perception is based on experience, which never seems to remain with Adams. Indeed, Adams' argument with the host represents two kinds of learning—one nursed not merely on books, but narrowly on "Plato and Seneca for that," and the other, the robust practicality of a seafaring man. The host has learned from his own unfortunate experience with this gentleman, and his down-to-earth attitude is reflected in his views on trade. Although Adams convincingly expands his metaphor to emphasize the importance of spiritual nourishment, we should remember that the host has just demonstrated the essentially practical nature of charity in which Fielding believes so strongly. Both Adams and the host are fine men —but it is their failings which give a sense of life to this particular conversation.

BOOK III

Chapter 1

Summary

In contrasting biographers with those "romance-writers who entitle their books "The History of England" . . . etc.," Fielding states that biographers always grasp the *human* truth, if not the truth of the details of an age or a country. But, while praising biographers, he observes that they copy nature instead of creating their own originals "from the confused heap of matter in their own brains." Taking *Don Quixote* as an example, Fielding claims that there is a timeless quality about such works and applies this principle to *Joseph Andrews,* in which he claims to describe "not men, but manners; not an individual, but a species." Thus Fielding avoids libelling an individual and, by satirizing timeless human traits, he holds up a mirror to us all.

Commentary

In the introduction to Book III, Fielding reminds the reader of the purpose of this novel. He dismisses historians, who emphasize the trappings of mankind, and "authors of immense romances," who spin out their own fantasies; in contrast, he praises the creative approach remarkably similar to that proposed by the poet Imlac in Chapter 10 of Dr. Johnson's *Rasselas:*

> "The business of a poet," said Imlac, "is to examine, not the individual, but the species; to remark general properties and large appearances; he does not number the streaks of the tulip, or describe the different shades in the verdure of the forest. He is to exhibit in his portraits of nature such prominent and striking features as recall the original to every mind. . . . He must write as the interpreter of nature and the legislator of mankind, and consider himself as presiding over the thoughts and manner of future generations, as a being superior to time and place."

Such an approach enables Fielding to address his remarks to men of all times, and although the "streaks of the tulip" may be missing, the portraits are nonetheless taken from life. In asserting that he has described no more than he has seen, Fielding echoes his remark in the preface that "life everywhere furnishes an accurate observer with the ridiculous." This cool and chiselled appraisal of the purpose and direction of the novel, carefully placed midway and reinforcing the arguments of the preface again indicates Fielding's control of his craft.

He describes what he sees, not what he imagines; his glance encompasses earth rather than heaven. Nonetheless his nose is not so close to the mire (which Parson Adams falls into) that he misses the heavenly qualities of true charity, toward which our moral sense is directed.

Chapter 2

Summary

Night overtakes the travellers as they take a rest by the roadside but before long, they see some "vanishing" lights and hear voices conspiring to murder someone. Adams thinks it must be ghosts, but is nevertheless determined to battle their ethereal matter with his crabstick. Joseph however persuades him that it would be wiser to flee. Finally, they arrive at a house where they are courteously treated by a "plain kind of man" and his hospitable wife. They talk for a while, then are startled by a loud knocking on the door. Adams mutters about spirits being abroad, but their host returns, saying that the "murderers" are no more than sheep stealers, now apprehended by some shepherds. The master of the house, uncertain of the relationship between the three, sounds out Adams, and his questions lead to a panegyric from Adams (after a lament for his lost copy of Aeschylus) on Homer's *Iliad*. In concluding, Adams thunders out a hundred verses in Greek. The host wonders if he might not have a bishop present and offers them food and lodging, and later, when his wife and the exhausted Fanny have retired, produces a bottle of his best beer as the men draw their chairs round the fireside. Adams then recounts Joseph's life history and asks their host to return the favor with the story of his own life.

Commentary

This chapter both increases our understanding of Adams and introduces us to Mr. Wilson, whose account of his own life contains many of the major themes of the book. Adams is comically superstitious, but brave; he does not fully understand what is confronting him in the night, but advances to the attack anyway. Joseph's pragmatism is in contrast to Adams' immediate, sincere, but mistaken responses: a penknife is more practical than a prayer and retreat is safer than attack; Adams falls head over heels down a hill, while Joseph walks down it firmly and safely; and Adams would swim across a river while Joseph quietly suggests walking farther along to a bridge. All this low comedy cannot match the gem of the chapter — Adams' sensitive and inspired discussion of Homer's *Iliad*. His profound appreciation of the *Iliad* is pertinent to *Joseph Andrews* itself; Adams remarks particularly on Homer's achievement in terms of the "*Harmotton*, that agreement of his action to his subject: for, as the subject is anger, how agreeable is his action, which is war; from which every incident arises, and to which every episode immediately relates." It is this same unity of theme which characterizes *Joseph Andrews*. Mr. Wilson is as fortuitously introduced into the narrative as was Fanny, but already his character is filling out some of the main themes of the book. He is a "plain kind of man" whose instincts are warm toward the travellers, but who is nevertheless prudent enough to make sure of the facts that lie beneath their appearance. His generosity is sincere and complete, and is akin to the charity of Adams. His life story relates closely to the book as a whole, and Adams' eagerness to hear it (one remembers his rapt attention to the story of Leonora) is a ripple of curiosity on the surface of the narrative that indicates the deep satisfaction and fulfillment which Adams gains from books and which has been so well revealed in his appreciation of the classics.

Chapter 3

Summary

Wilson relates his history. His father died when Wilson was only sixteen, and claiming his modest inheritance prematurely,

Wilson left for London. He set out to be a "fine gentleman" and is soon indulging in all the surface vanities and fopperies of this kind of life—although the groaning Adams would hardly call it "life," referring to it instead as an existence beneath that of an animal. Wilson relates that after two years the prospect of a duel forced him to move to the Temple, which is simply a less prestigious environment for the same sort of life. Despite some worthy resolutions induced by bouts of venereal disease, he engaged in one affair after the other, popping back and forth between mistress and surgeon. At this point, Wilson comments from his vantage point of maturity and roundly condemns vanity as the "worst of passions." Gamesters finished off Wilson's fortune and haunted by debts, he turned to play-writing, but was met by coldness from his friends, refusals from patrons, and prevarications from the theater managers. Eventually Wilson bought a lottery ticket with some savings from doing translations, but although the ticket won a prize of £3,000 it did nothing to relieve Wilson from his ill-health, penury, and being arrested for unpaid bills—for he had earlier sold the ticket for bread. Wilson was in prison and had abandoned all hope when he received a most sympathetic letter, enclosing £200, from the daughter and heiress of the man—now deceased—to whom he had sold the lottery ticket. Wilson had long nursed, but concealed, a passion for this Harriet Hearty, and in his profusions of gratitude, he declared his love for her. They were married soon after, but Wilson was too honest in his management of her father's wine trade to make any profit. He has seen that "the pleasures of the world are chiefly folly, and the business of it mostly knavery, and both nothing better than vanity." Thus, he retired with his wife and their diminished fortune from the scamper and scurry of the world to the peace of their present home. No happiness is unalloyed, however, and Mr. Wilson finishes his life history by relating the loss of his eldest son, stolen many years ago from his door by gypsies.

Commentary

The early life of Wilson represents somewhat Fielding's version of Hogarth's graphic portrayal of The Rake's Progress.

Although the history is complete in itself and contains a gallery of characters who do not play any other part in *Joseph Andrews*, the theme of the account is central to Fielding's larger purpose; in the Leonora digression, we read of the contrast between affectation, hypocrisy, vanity, and the even rhythm of true values and charity. Wilson's early concern was with a "tailor, a periwig-maker, and some few more tradesmen, who deal in furnishing out the human body." The town—as we observed in the Lady Booby incidents—thrives on surface values, and it is not until Wilson and his wife have retired to the country that they find true happiness. Jonathan Swift would have flailed such a coquette as Sapphira; compare Fielding's treatment of her with Swift's description of a Yahoo coquette in Book IV of *Gulliver's Travels*. But Fielding is always positive, and against the wretchedness of town life, he proposes the charity of Harriet Hearty, the honesty—however belated—which she inspires in Wilson, and the reaction of Adams. As in the Leonora episode (the end of which poor Adams never heard!), Adams reacts in the simplest and most genuine way. His groans swell and diminish according to the degree of worldliness in the story, but when he is pleased at a turn of events he rapturously snaps his fingers. He interjects lengthy moral comments and once again reveals his complete involvement in the process of listening to a story; we should be responding to Fielding's narrative with the same sincerity and eagerness. But Adams is no perfect example; however much he may agree with Wilson that "vanity is the worst of passions," his insistence on the surpassing merit of his own sermon against vanity is a delightful irony which neither we nor Mr. Wilson can ignore.

Chapter 4

Summary and Commentary

Adams indulges his fantasy as to the possible identity of Wilson's lost son, but Wilson asserts that he would know him among ten thousand, as he has a strawberry-shaped birthmark on the left side of his chest. Wilson then takes Adams and Joseph outside to show them his garden, where he now spends much of his time, and tells them of his present, peaceful way of life. Both the bliss which Wilson experiences in his family and in tending his garden contrast strongly with his earlier life. But the needless shooting of his daughter's favorite dog shows that the harsh outside world does impinge even on this haven of happiness.

Chapter 5

Summary and Commentary

The three travellers, rested and refreshed, take their leave of the Wilsons. In discussing Mr. Wilson, Adams blames his early dissipation on his public school education; Joseph disagrees, maintaining that a public school education gives one a better preparation for the world than private education does. Adams' enthusiasm for the latter is based partly on his desire to preserve the innocence of children; ironically, however, Adams' own simple and innocent nature bears out Joseph's assertion that inherent dispositions will predominate, whatever the external influence on them. The discussion ends when they decide to have a picnic lunch in a delightful spot. Adams discovers a piece of gold which Mr. Wilson has put amongst their provisions, and Fielding provides himself with another thread for his final knot by linking Adams' wish to repay Mr. Wilson with the gratifying prospect of the visit that Mr. Wilson is to make within the week to Adams' parish.

Chapters 6-9

Summary

In a long monologue on charity (a monologue because Adams is asleep), Joseph maintains that the desire for honor should lead man, not to material acquisition—one's possessions are so often criticized behind one's back—but to charity: "I defy the wisest man in the world to turn a true good action into ridicule." Noticing that Adams is asleep, Joseph turns from his philosophizing to matters more of this world, but Fanny's tenderhearted reaction to the beleaguered hare that interrupts their dalliance continues the theme of charity. For all Fanny's pity, the hare is finally caught by the hounds and killed before her eyes; in fact, the hare is so close to Adams that some of the hounds start to pull his cassock to bits. Adams flees, but the master of the pack sets his hounds in pursuit. As the hounds close in on Adams, however, Joseph is there with his cudgel, and the pair of them defend themselves with such success that the master of the hunt calls off his bruised and battered pack. The gentleman's fury is mollified only by the appearance of Fanny, and he invites the travellers to dinner with more devious and wicked thoughts than revenge in his head. His attempts to further these by stupefying Adams and Joseph with drink perhaps have something to do with his upbringing. He has been privately educated, and in this, as well as in his travels and his career in Parliament, the squire has followed his own whims and penchant for the grotesque; indeed, his companions are closer to curs than are his hounds. The squire's strange retinue taunts Adams in a truly cur-like way, and Adams berates the squire for turning a blind eye to the grossly inhospitable behavior of the poet, the player, and the dancing-master. The hypocritical doctor takes the side of Adams, but the trick with which he replaces the buffoonery of the others differs only in its skillful disguise: Adams finds himself in a tub of water instead of on a throne. Furious, he dunks the squire and leaves with Joseph and Fanny, which infuriates the squire. He sends his cronies in fast pursuit.

Adams, Joseph, and Fanny come to an inn, where Adams falls into a conversation with a Roman Catholic priest, who ends his long tirade on the evil of money with a request to Adams for a loan. To Adams' consternation, he finds that he has lost all his money, but this doesn't stop him from taking comfort in the simple and homely provisions of the inn. This peace is short-lived, however; the morning brings with it the captain, the poet and the player in pursuit of Fanny. A battle royal ensues and the end of it all is that Fanny is carried off while the soiled Adams and the stunned Joseph are tied to the bedposts.

Commentary

Joseph's comments on charity preface a sour and brutal episode. We may laugh at Adams as he becomes a "hare" for the hounds, and the assault on Adams by the dogs may be burlesque, but already Adams' human assailants are being referred to as animals. The squire's bestial lust and the malicious behavior of his court of assorted brutes are entirely devoid of humanity. Again Adams judges others by his own "inoffensive disposition," and is an easy prey both for the squire's cranks and for the hypocritical Catholic. He is most at home with simple things, whether it be the physical valor that saves him from the squire or the homely bed that restores his strength sufficiently to allow him to fight again with equal vigor the next day.

Chapter 10

Summary and Commentary

The poet and the player engage in a discussion on the respective merits and faults of their fellow artists. Both are angling for compliments and scraping together what they can to restore their shattered egos. At first they find they can form an alliance with vanity; each vilifies all other poets or players as the case may be, but praises his companion. This pretence crumbles, however, when the player proves unable to repeat a speech from one of the poet's plays, and they fall to attacking each other. Each is as much of a hack as the other, but both are so convinced of their virtuosity that the argument would have gone on forever had Fielding not put an end to his digression, which he has compared to a dramatic interlude.

Chapter 11

Summary and Commentary

The full impact of the abduction of Fanny now hits Joseph, and he gives passionate vent to his grief, much to the consternation of Parson Adams, still firmly tied to the other bedpost.

Adams lectures Joseph severely on the necessity of summoning reason, patience, and submission to his aid. None of this is of any comfort to Joseph, who simply wants Fanny back in his arms.

Adams never falters in his actions, but when he tries to theorize he loses a relation with reality; fortunately, his own reactions in a similar situation in Book IV, Chapter 8, bear little relation to his Stoic theories, which here miss the mark though they stem from the best of motives. Still, his quotations about the folly of grief are as incongruous as Joseph's quotation is heartfelt and to the point:

> Yes, I will bear my sorrows like a man,
> But I must also feel them as a man.

Still Adams responds unfavorably; he disapproves of drama, and Macduff's lament (see *Macbeth,* IV.iii.220-26 for the correct version) passes him by.

Chapters 12-13

Summary

The captain carries away the terrified Fanny, reminding her with relish that she will soon be a virgin no more. A passing traveller ignores her anguish, but two armed horsemen appear, one of whom recognizes Fanny. The carriage they are attending arrives, and on the strength of Fanny's entreaties and the support of the horseman, the gentleman—none other than Mr. Peter Pounce, preceding his mistress, Lady Booby, on her return from London—takes Fanny into his carriage. They arrive back at the inn where the poet and the player are berating each other downstairs while Adams and Joseph talk back to back upstairs. Joseph, after a rapturous reunion with Fanny, gives the captain a drubbing he will never forget (the poet and the player once again join forces and share a horse to escape); Adams tidies himself up, Pounce has something to eat, and the innkeeper's wife does her best to make amends for the hostile behavior of her "block-head" husband. Later, they all set out for Booby-Hall, with Adams travelling in the coach with Pounce. But in the course of their conversation it becomes clear that Pounce and the Parson have very different notions of charity; Pounce will admit a disposition toward charity, but not the act itself, and indeed hates the poor as soon as he loses a penny to them. In his smug and selfish wealth, Pounce deeply offends Adams, who jumps out of the carriage and proceeds on foot beside Fanny and Joseph to Booby-Hall.

Commentary

Fielding moves from one episode to the next, openly declaring his manipulation, yet is able, without a sense of strain, to resolve things at the inn where Adams, Joseph, the poet, and the player are pursuing their various lines of argument. He is now collecting all the threads together; the travels of Adams, Joseph, and Fanny are almost over, and the other characters are converging on the Booby estate as Fielding prepares for the final scenes.

Peter Pounce is as avaricious as ever (see Book I, Chapter 10) and more than a little lustful. Yet his worst evil is his selfish and complacent attitude. In the altercation between Adams and Pounce we are again reminded that charity must be actively pursued; Adams' abrupt exit from the carriage is a reassuring reminder that he *acts* on his beliefs.

BOOK IV

Chapters 1-3

Summary

Lady Booby returns home and the sight of Joseph once again sets her passion rioting against her reason. After an agitated night, she summons Mrs. Slipslop and asks for an account of Joseph's dismissal and departure. Mrs. Slipslop, however, begins to praise the handsome, young Joseph, and the two women engage in another jealous tiff.

When Lady Booby attends church the next day, her ogling of Joseph is interrupted by Adams' announcement of the banns of marriage between Joseph and Fanny. Furious, Lady Booby summons Adams and condemns the character of the two lovers, but Adams stands firm in his approval of the match, despite Lady Booby's threats to have him dismissed. Moreover, she is alarmed by what Adams has learned from lawyer Scout: any person who serves a year gains a settlement in the parish where he serves. She sends for this potentially dangerous lawyer. Unlike Adams, however, Scout quickly bends himself to Lady Booby's purpose; he echoes her reasoning, vilifies Fanny, and refers her to Justice Frolick as the man to legally exterminate the two. Fielding closes by saying that the vermin who eat up the poor committed to Bridewell are really none other than the Scouts of this world, who are the "pests of society."

Commentary

The turbulence of Lady Booby's emotions is strikingly shown by the way that Adams' reference to Fanny's beauty lodges itself in her distracted mind, which feasts with a strange fascination on this poisonous piece of knowledge.

The steadfast honesty of Adams stands in direct contrast to the sly hypocrisy of Scout, who will ensure—for certain favors—that no law stands in the way of the will of such eminent people as Lady Booby.

Chapters 4-6

Summary

On Tuesday, two days after her interviews with Adams and Scout, Lady Booby is returning from church, where she has just heard the second publication of the banns. To her further dismay she now learns from Slipslop that Scout has carried *both* Fanny and Joseph before the justice. Earlier, she wanted to be rid of them both, but now she cannot bear to lose Joseph. Her worries are interrupted, however, by the arrival of her nephew and his wife, Pamela (who is Joseph's sister). News of Joseph's arrest reaches Mr. Booby through his servants, and he leaves to see what he can do to help his brother-in-law. He arrives at the "judgment-seat" just after the justice, who is a neighbor and an acquaintance of his, has ordered Joseph and Fanny to Bridewell for a month. Mr. Booby reads the deposition, written by the justice himself, and is horrified to find that the trumped-up charge is no more than that "Joseph Andrews with a nife cut one hassel-twig" belonging to lawyer Scout, who smugly remarks that "if we had called it a young tree, they would have been both hanged." Booby protests and the justice commits Joseph and Fanny to Mr. Booby's custody. When Joseph is dressed in a suit of Mr. Booby's, the three return in Mr. Booby's coach and meet Parson Adams on his way to rescue his two parishioners. Lady Booby is delighted to learn that Joseph has become a member of the family, but she will not tolerate the presence of Fanny, who departs with Adams. Joseph joyfully meets his sister, but at the end of his account of his adventures, he is dismayed to find that he is expected to spend the night at Lady Booby's. Late that night, Lady Booby talks to Slipslop about her various doubts and passions, and Slipslop dutifully echoes Lady Booby's vilification of Fanny and her fulsome praise of Joseph. She is a little too direct, however, in her encouragement to the "lady of fashion" to marry Joseph. Lady Booby is highly indignant, but Slipslop merely laughs at her mistress and bids her goodnight.

Commentary

The justice, like Scout, is a miserably inadequate man of law; illiterate and open to pressure, he is prepared to initiate any charge simply to satisfy Lady Booby—and is equally prepared to drop it to accommodate Mr. Booby.

It is vanity that leads Mr. Booby to dress up his brother-in-law for presentation to Lady Booby, who is delighted to see Joseph again. The novel has come full circle; at the beginning, Joseph was stripped of his livery, now he is being clothed. Significantly, he chooses "the plainest dress he could find," his genteel appearance stemming not so much from the superficial perfection of fit, but from Joseph's own essential qualities: "no person would have doubted its being as well adapted to his quality as his shape."

Chapter 7

Summary

Fielding inserts a lengthy discussion on the "practisers of deceit" and the attitudes about love that young ladies are reared with. This helps explain Lady Booby's confusion in her relationship with Joseph. She has been taught that the more she loves a man, the more she should "counterfeit the antipathy."

Continuing with the narrative, we see Lady Booby prompting her nephew to try to dissuade Joseph from his match with Fanny—which would further relate the Booby family to "inferior creatures." But Joseph is adamant in his attachment to Fanny, even though Pamela joins Mr. Booby in discouraging him. Meanwhile, Fanny is assaulted—first, by a young gentleman and then by his servant. But "the deity who presides over chaste love" brings Joseph to her rescue. Recovering from the battle—and seeing "the snowy hue of Fanny's bosom," Joseph sets off with Fanny for the house of Parson Adams.

Commentary

Fielding's comments on the way in which girls accommodate themselves to not only the idea, but also the practice of "love" bear on the novel's central theme of deception; by deceiving others, women deceive themselves the most. While Lady Booby clearly wants Joseph for herself (although she deceives herself that she hates this mere footman), her nephew agrees to persuade Joseph to break off with Fanny out of pride for the family. It is disturbing to find Pamela also a part of this vanity and snobbishness; in marrying Mr. Booby, she feels that the name of Andrews is now beneath her social rank. Hypocritical and ambitious beneath her modest exterior, Pamela is now echoing Richardson's original. Joseph's love for Fanny is admirable in its unselfishness and self-control, but Fielding's gentle humor as he describes the confused, sexually aroused pair at the close of the chapter shows that we must not take the theme of chastity too ponderously.

Chapter 8

Summary

Joseph and Fanny arrive just as Mrs. Adams — as always, having the last word — concludes a quarrel with her husband, whom she has been berating for opposing Lady Booby. Mrs. Adams recognizes the power of Lady Booby's influence and she knows what is necessary for the material advancement of her children. But Adams is much more concerned with his moral duty than with worldly interests, and when Joseph, alarmed by his recent experiences, asks to be immediately married, Adams lectures him severely on impatience and fear. Despite his insistence that "we must submit in all things to the will of Providence," and his reference to Abraham's Stoic qualities in accepting the sacrifice of his son, Adams is demented by the sudden news that his youngest son has drowned. Joseph attempts in vain to comfort Adams by employing many of the parson's own arguments against passion, when suddenly Jacky (Dick) himself appears, bedraggled but alive, thanks to his timely rescue by the same peddler who had previously aided his father. Adams is as overcome with joy as he had been previously with grief, and his admonition to Joseph not to give way to his passions is not convincing. He tries to justify himself by distinguishing between filial and marital love, which occasions a sharp retort from his wife, who says that Adams hardly practices what he preaches; he has been a "loving and cherishing husband" to her.

Commentary

It is clear that Adams thinks of his children with less practical interest than does his wife, but with just as much love, as his outburst of grief shows. His feelings quite belie the theories he expresses here and in Book III, Chapter 11, but this inconsistency only makes him more human. Trained in the ways of philosophy and proud of his abilities as a teacher, Adams nevertheless expands beyond this framework with the "overflowings of a full, honest, open heart."

Note how the peddler, who is to play a vital part in the final intricacies of the plot, is re-introduced, again through an act of charity.

Chapters 9-11

Summary

Lady Booby arrives with her entourage at Parson Adams', taking the cluttered Adams household quite by surprise; her purpose is to reunite Fanny as firmly as possible with her gentleman assailant, who on his arrival at Booby-Hall gave Lady Booby a rapturous account of his encounter with Fanny. The gentleman's name is Beau Didapper, and in mind and body, he resembles a stunted insect. While he flirts with Fanny, Lady Booby asks to hear the parson's son read a little. Dick is somewhat confused by his father's request in Latin, but after some testy prompting, he begins to read the history of Leonard and his wife, who were a quarreling pair frequently greeted by Paul, an old friend. Paul patches over their quarrels by secretly assuring each one that theirs is the right side in whatever dispute arises, and that the person who is right should always submit. What happens when Leonard and his wife discover this secret diplomacy, we never learn for the history is interrupted when Joseph notices Didapper trying to lay hold of Fanny. He promptly boxes him on the ear, and chaos ensues. They exchange loud blows, while Lady Booby upbraids Joseph for defending such a wench as Fanny. Adams springs to Joseph's defense, fully armed with the lid of a pan. Mr. Booby and Pamela add their comments about the impropriety of the match, and the two men are finally parted. Joseph leaves, bearing Fanny with him. He is soon followed by Lady Booby and company, after which Adams is berated by his wife and daughter. Joseph returns then with Fanny and the peddler who saved Dick from drowning and invites the Adams family to dinner; despite her recent harsh words, Mrs. Adams accepts readily, pleased to be relieved of providing for them all.

Commentary

Fielding told us in the preface that anyone who looked on poverty as being ridiculous in itself "hath a very ill-framed mind"; Lady Booby's attitude of contempt toward Adams and his impoverished household hardly measures up to the sincere welcome which Adams gives to his unexpected guests. And, while we have read previously of Adams' vanity as a teacher, then observe poor Dick at a loss with his Latin, it is much more important to recognize the sense of charity which the son has clearly learned from his father. Joseph's generosity in his gift of a shilling to Dick also reveals the parson's influence. Indeed, Joseph's conduct now has a new courage and assurance which have been slowly developing throughout the book.

Chapters 12-14

Summary

The peddler has been doing some detective work and, having discovered that Fanny was bought by Sir Thomas Booby when she was three or four years old, he is now able to reveal Fanny's family name. In his days as a drummer, the peddler had kept a mistress, who confessed on her deathbed of an incident that happened long ago while she was travelling with some gypsies. Apparently she stole a child and then sold it to Sir Thomas. The true parents of this child, the peddler says, were none other than Mr. and Mrs. Andrews—Joseph's parents! The consternation is enormous: Joseph is in love with his sister!

Meanwhile, in the privacy of Lady Booby's chamber, Slipslop arrives with the news that Joseph and Fanny are now thought to be brother and sister. Everyone assembles at Booby-Hall, where the peddler repeats his tale; the doubts, we learn, will be resolved next day by the Andrewses themselves when they come to collect Pamela and Mr. Booby.

At dinner, Adams is in excellent form and provides some highlights later as well. Beau Didapper, amorously on the prowl for Fanny, jumps by mistake into the bed of Slipslop, who decides to bolster her sagging reputation by screaming out that she is being raped. Adams races instantly and nakedly to the rescue, but lands his blows on the bearded chin of Slipslop while the smooth-skinned Didapper darts away. Lady Booby arrives on the scene to find Slipslop held fast by her breasts, and she immediately assumes that the naked Adams has been occupied in obliging her. The embarrassed Adams whips under the sheets, and the confusion begins to clear when Lady Booby finds the remains of Beau Didapper's shirt and diamond cuff links on the floor. Lady Booby leaves, and Adams follows. But Adams is so tired and confused that he enters the wrong room and curls up in Fanny's bed, where Joseph is somewhat surprised to find him when he enters in the morning. Poor Fanny is chagrined, and Adams thinks that witches are working on him, but soon all is resolved, and Joseph guides the erring Adams back to his own room.

Commentary

The initial discovery that Fanny appears to be his sister is of course confusing to Joseph, but it is only one pull of the string from an author who has constantly been in complete control. Joseph's control is also growing; he steers the erring Adams back to his own bedroom, and while Adams rejoices that incest between Joseph and Fanny has been avoided and mutters about witchcraft, we feel that the resolution engineered by Fielding's reason and clear-sightedness is just around the corner.

Chapters 15-16

Summary

Gaffar and Gammar Andrews arrive shortly after breakfast, and though Mr. Andrews denies that Fanny is his daughter, his wife confirms the peddler's story. Fanny, she says, was born when Mr. Andrews had been with the army in Gibraltar, and had been stolen by gypsies, who had left Joseph in Fanny's cradle. Mrs. Andrews raised Joseph as her own, and on his return from Gibraltar, Gaffar had not suspected that anything was amiss.

On hearing this, the peddler is curious to know whether Joseph has a birthmark, and Mrs. Andrews affirms that he bears the mark of a strawberry on his breast. Something stirs in Adams' memory, but it is the peddler who tells Joseph that his parents are "persons of much greater circumstances than those he had hitherto mistaken for such; for that he had been stolen from a gentleman's house by those whom they call gypsies."

Mr. Wilson now arrives for his promised visit to Adams' parish, and on hearing the peddler's story, demands to see Joseph's birthmark. It is true: Mr. Wilson is none other than Joseph's father. Joseph receives his father's joyful blessing while the frustrated Lady Booby leaves the room in anguish.

The company travels to the country house of Mr. Booby, where a happy Mrs. Wilson joins them. Joseph and Fanny are married by Parson Adams and retire to live on a small estate purchased with the £2,000 which Mr. Booby gave to Fanny. Mr. Booby also gives Adams a decent living and sees to it that the peddler is made an exciseman. Lady Booby returns to London, where the combination of cards and a young captain soon obliterates the memory of Joseph.

Commentary

Joseph and Fanny settle in the country, the movement away from the town is complete; indeed, the social order is re-aligned in a manner typical of a Shakespearian comedy, where people find their true natures and their destiny after much confusion and wandering. The same sense of destiny has guided Joseph after his dismissal from Lady Booby's household to his true home and identity, and the Wilsons and Mr. and Mrs. Booby have also found themselves, the former in their happiness in their restored son, the latter in their "old English hospitality," which represents a genuine transformation in their characters. Justice is also done as we learn that the thief who assaulted Fanny as she was journeying to meet Joseph has been committed to Salisbury gaol. The end is Shakespearian too in that some things continue to be the same: Adams will always fall off his horse; Gaffar Andrews wants no more children than he can keep and is more interested in his pipe than in Fanny; and Lady Booby remains outside the readjusted scheme of things.

The fairy tale ending is an aspect of Fielding's control of his craft. The marriage of Joseph and Fanny may be contrived and idealistic, but it is sincere and unadorned; its order answers to what man wants to be and its simplicity to what man is. It is apt that Fielding closes his story with the clothing metaphor which has been so important throughout in revealing man for what he is: Joseph "refused all finery; as did Fanny likewise, who could be prevailed on by Pamela to attire herself in nothing richer than a white dimity nightgown."

CHARACTER ANALYSES

JOSEPH ANDREWS

Joseph's chief attributes are his self-control, his virtue, and his devotion. He is attractive physically, as Lady Booby and Mrs. Slipslop are well aware, and his character matches this exterior excellence. The strength of his pure love for Fanny Goodwill enables him to deal plainly, directly, and even violently with the moral and physical weaklings who cross his path, be it the lustful Lady Booby or the insect of a man, Beau Didapper. Joseph is a man of genuine emotion, and it is this which inspires him to the virtuous *action* which Fielding believed so important: "I defy the wisest man in the world to turn a true good action into ridicule," Joseph comments in Book III. Joseph, however, would be a bore if he were only a knight-like figure. Fielding enhances his moralizing by giving us much rich laughter. It is true that Joseph is always ready to do battle for a stranger, but, throughout the novel, Joseph battles most for his chastity and it is this satiric reversal which is the basis of Fielding's "comic epic-poem."

FANNY

As with Joseph, Fanny's outward beauty is matched by her inner qualities. She has sensibility, sweetness, and gentility; in short, she is the perfect object for Joseph's love, and the way in which she immediately takes to the road in search of Joseph after hearing of his plight testifies that she too has a depth of feeling all too rare in this novel. Yet she also possesses a deep sense of modesty; and, in all honesty, one must admit that Fanny is a little too perfect. But part of her charm is in the way Fielding uses her in his comic contrasts. Whether we are seeing Mrs. Slipslop huffily "forgetting" the name of this "impertinent" girl, or Lady Booby plagued to distraction by the mention of Fanny's beauty, the emphasis is on Fielding's satire of hypocrisy rather than on Fanny's pristine goodness itself.

LADY BOOBY

Lady Booby is everything that Joseph and Fanny are not; attached to town life, blind to her own motives and consequently to those of others, shallow in her feelings and thus scornful of those who do feel deeply, her dangerous legal maneuvers in Book IV have extremely unpleasant implications.

Throughout the novel, Lady Booby's reason and her passion are at odds; she is clearly the agent of confusion in Fielding's comic plan. Her mental muddle works against the resolution toward which he is drawing his characters, her selfishness denies the love on which this resolution is based, and her concern for her reputation exile her from the novel's happy ending. Yet the energy and vividness with which Lady Booby is portrayed in her turmoils prevent us from seeing her as a supreme villainess; she is more than a pawn in Fielding's game. She embodies the struggles which we all have at times: "I despise, I detest my passions. Yet why?"

MRS. SLIPSLOP

At the beginning of Chapter 5 (Book I), Fielding points out that he often uses Slipslop as a foil to her mistress, Lady Booby. By making them both fall for Joseph, Fielding can point out the "different operations of this passion of love in the gentle and cultivated mind of Lady Booby, from those which it effected in the less-polished disposition of Mrs. Slipslop." Slipslop is a foil and also a coarse echo of Lady Booby; she is vain and proud and thus is "a mighty affecter of hard words" toward those whom she considers her inferiors, such as Mrs. Grave-airs and Fanny Goodwill. Yet there are also crucial differences between Slipslop and her mistress. Slipslop is ridiculous in a warm way; we laugh kindly at the incongruity of a fat, pimply, red-faced, lame, forty-five-year-old slob pursuing Joseph. But at least she is direct in her physical desires; when Adams mistakenly enters her bed, she realizes that he is not Joseph, but that he is better than nothing. Lady Booby could never do this. Slipslop may be a snob in some matters, but she is always superbly practical.

PARSON ADAMS

Adams is a very good man and yet a very human man; he has his head in the clouds and although his feet are on the ground, they are usually in puddles. Comic though he is, he is the firm pivot of the novel's moral influence. It is his belief in charitable *action* which distinguishes him as a parson from such hypocritical boors as Trulliber. Like Joseph and Fanny, he acts on his feelings, and it is because of this affinity that he is such a fine guardian and guide to the young pair.

The devious ways of the world wash off Adams as surely as the filth of the pigsty or the muck of the chamber pot, for he trusts his learning to books. This unchanging quality of innocence — will Adams never learn about money? — is part of Adams' worth as a character. Throughout the novel, he never develops, never changes, but we know what he stands for; he is ever active, ever charitable.

REVIEW QUESTIONS

1. What factors influenced Fielding in his conception and composition of *Joseph Andrews?*

2. What is the purpose of the *Author's Preface,* and how well did Fielding accomplish his aims in the light of the guidelines established there?

3. Examine one or two incidents or scenes which you think were influenced in their creation by Fielding's experience as a playwright; what is 'dramatic' about the scenes you have chosen, and is there a place for this kind of effect in the novel?

4. To what use does Fielding put his love and knowledge of the classics?

5. Discuss the function of the "digressions" in *Joseph Andrews.*

6. Discuss the degree of unity or—to use Fielding's terms— "*Harmotton*, that agreement of his action to his subject" (Book III, Chapter 2) achieved in *Joseph Andrews.*

7. "I describe not men, but manners; not an individual, but a species" (Book III, Chapter 1). Discuss Fielding's presentation of two or three characters in the light of the above comment.

8. Compare the hypocrisy of Lady Booby with that of Mrs. Slipslop.

9. Do you agree with Fielding that the character of Adams "is the most glaring in the whole"? Give your reasons and discuss the implications.

10. Compare and contrast the attitudes of two or three characters toward "charity."

11. To what end does Fielding contrast town life and country life?

12. "I defy the wisest man in the world to turn a true good action into ridicule" (Book III, Chapter 6). To what extent is this statement the fulcrum of *Joseph Andrews?*

13. Cite some examples of Fielding's use of the burlesque and discuss the use of this kind of humor in *Joseph Andrews.*

14. What does Fielding mean when he speaks of the "ridiculous"? Give an example of the "ridiculous" and discuss Fielding's treatment of it.

15. Discuss Fielding's presentation of clergymen; what do you believe to be his conception of the truly worthy man of religion?

16. What kind of picture does Fielding paint of "law and justice" in eighteenth-century England?

SELECTED BIBLIOGRAPHY

Books

BATTESTIN, MARTIN C. (ed.) *Joseph Andrews and Shamela.* London: Methuen, 1965. See the introduction—an excellent discussion of the relationship of the two works.

————. *The Moral Basis of Fielding's Art: A Study of "Joseph Andrews."* Middletown, Conn.: Wesleyan Univ. Press, 1959. A perceptive account of the religious and philosophical background to Fielding's choice of such heroes as Joseph Andrews and Parson Adams.

BUTT, JOHN. *Fielding.* London: Longmans, 1954. The best short introduction to Fielding.

JENKINS, ELIZABETH. *Henry Fielding*. London: Arthur Barker, 1966. A short and lively critical biography.

MACALLISTER, HAMILTON. *Fielding*. London: Evans Brothers, 1967. A plain-spoken account of Fielding the writer and man, with detailed chapters on the sources, structure, characters, and themes of *Joseph Andrews*.

PAULSON, R. (ed.). *Fielding: A Collection of Critical Essays*. Englewood Cliffs, N.J.: Prentice-Hall, 1962. An introduction followed by thirteen essays by modern critics.

WRIGHT, A. *Henry Fielding: Mask and Feast*. London: Chatto and Windus, 1965. A useful general study.

Articles

BATTESTIN, MARTIN C. "Fielding's Changing Politics and *Joseph Andrews*," *Philological Quarterly*, XXXIX (1960), 39-55.

CAUTHEN, I. B., JR. "Fielding's Digressions in *Joseph Andrews*," *College English*, XVII (April 1956), 379-82.

SPILKA, MARK. "Comic Resolution in Fielding's *Joseph Andrews*," *College English*, XV (October 1953), 11-19.

TAYLOR, DICK, JR. "Joseph as Hero of *Joseph Andrews*," *Tulane Studies in English*, VII (1957), 91-109.

NOTES

NOTES

NOTES

NOTES

NOTES

NOTES

NOTES